Best Laid Plans

A Simple Planning System for Living a Life That You Love

Sarah Hart-Unger

Published by Sourcebooks
1935 Brookdale RD, Naperville, IL 60563-2773
(630) 961-3900
sourcebooks.com

Cataloging-in-Publication Data is on file with the Library of Congress.

Printed and bound in the United States of America.
KP 10 9 8 7 6 5 4 3 2

Praise for *Best Laid Plans*

"*Best Laid Plans* is a masterclass in planning—thoughtful, thorough, and deeply kind. Ideas abound for the organizational newbie and aficionado alike. If you enjoy planning even a little, you will devour this book."

—Kendra Adachi, *New York Times* bestselling author of *The Lazy Genius Way*, *The Lazy Genius Kitchen*, and *The PLAN*

"In this book, Sarah offers something both rare and sorely needed in our current productivity literature: an approach to time management designed for real people with real lives."

—Cal Newport, *New York Times* bestselling author of *Slow Productivity* and *Deep Work*

"The only plan you'll need to stop hating Mondays. Sarah Hart-Unger turns chaos into calm—without needing more hours in the day."

—Jodi Wellman, author of *You Only Die Once*

"I'll confess to being a planning skeptic, having tried too many systems promising infinite productivity while delivering only extra stress (and eating up time, because of how much work it took to administer them). But Sarah Hart-Unger's uniquely thoughtful approach points the way to a life of calm intentionality, grounded in the reality of our human limitations, yet focused on the accomplishments and experiences that matter most."

—Oliver Burkeman, *New York Times* bestselling author of *4000 Weeks* and *Meditations for Mortals*

To my husband, Joshua, and my children, Annabel, Cameron, and Genevieve. I love planning with all of you!

Table of Contents

Foreword

Sarah Hart-Unger and I first started emailing back and forth in 2013. We'd been reading each other's blogs, and she volunteered to participate in a project of mine, which involved studying how professional women with kids spend their time. She noted that "from your writing I think we see eye-to-eye on many things related to time management." Namely, that it was quite possible to have a career you love, be a doting and involved parent, pursue hobbies intensely, get enough sleep, and have fun while doing it. I took one look at her schedule and thought, *Wow. This woman gets it.*

Over the years, I've loved seeing how Sarah has continued to fill her life with more wonderful things than most people think is possible. She provides excellent care to her patients. She is forever dreaming up adventures to try with her family. She has posted on her blog almost every day for twenty years. She has trained for and completed six marathons. I get book recommendations from her because she's generally read whatever the hot book is long before I've gotten around to it. I was thrilled when, in 2017, she made the time to go into business with me to produce the *Best of Both Worlds* podcast. Even though we talk all the time, when she launched the *Best Laid Plans* podcast in 2020, I still found myself learning new strategies every week (I also found myself spending a lot more money on planners and pens, and developing opinions on washi tape, but that is a different matter). Lest you think this all involves stark trade-offs and no downtime, I can assure you that she even makes time to watch *Dance Moms* and *White Lotus*.

Key to all of this is her very wise system of planning. Sarah thinks about what she'd like to do with her time. Then she holds herself accountable for allocating her hours toward all her interests. On any given day, she knows what is most important and she's thought through the logistics to make it happen. To be sure, life does not always go according to plan. For example, we once recorded a podcast episode when she was in a hotel room somewhere because her family was evacuated from south Florida for a hurricane. Then there are the more humdrum realities of rescheduled meetings and traffic. But her planning system seems to be as resilient as one of those Florida palm trees that can take all matter of wind without blowing over. I've laughed as I've read the occasional blog comment from someone who assumes this is all a house of cards about to topple. Nope. And she'll make time to answer that comment, too!

Now, in *Best Laid Plans*, she shares her strategies with the rest of us. In this lighthearted and gentle book, you'll learn how to capture all the random tasks and details that seem to bombard modern sorts. You'll learn how to dream big about all the things you want to accomplish in life. You'll learn how to turn those dreams into action items as you check in with your goals at different prescribed intervals. You'll learn to create an ideal week template, and then how to match each day's intentions to your available time and energy so you can be realistic about what will get done. The good news is that even if any given day isn't a festival of productivity, over the long run, we can do a lot.

What I really appreciate about Sarah is that despite her superwoman level of accomplishments, she is authentic about her own struggles. She has not actually manufactured extra hours in the day, and indeed she faces many of the same challenges that other people do. Medicine is not the world's most flexible job. On her clinical days, she is seeing patients for many hours back-to-back. When she's on call, she's dealing with medical emergencies in the middle of the night. She knows what it's like to have to reorganize a day after a call from the school nurse, or to have her morning delayed by a child's decision to put on shoes as slowly as possible (note: the shoes probably won't be lost. Sarah has systems for that. But at a certain point, you can't really put on other people's shoes for them!).

But she also shows what is possible within those constraints. Even if your work hours are set, you can plan to use the hours around your shifts to build joy into your life. Even if you can't control other people, you can build buffers into your schedule so that delays aren't disasters. Everything that needs to get done gets done in due course. And you can make space for your own fun, too.

I think the effectiveness of Sarah's approach was most obvious to me when I watched her deal with some schedule challenges recently. Her kids had worked hard to get into competitive sports programs that had practices until around 9 p.m. some nights. She wanted to support them in their endeavors, but she also gets up before 5 a.m. to log the miles necessary for her own athletic goals.

Some people would throw up their hands and declare that no one can have it all. Something would have to give! Others would decide they had no choice but to be frazzled and sleep deprived, and see their own enjoyment of life fall off a cliff.

Sarah, on the other hand, understood that this was simply a planning challenge to be solved. She could rework the morning routine 1–2 days a week so she could start later. She figured out how to share the late -night driving with other families (and other members of her own family). She built systems to streamline the turnaround from activities to kid bedtimes, and she plotted out her sleep hours as she built her ideal week template to make sure that she was in bed for the amount of time she needed to be as well. As a result, everyone got to pursue their dreams without the hard trade-offs lots of people might think are required.

Plans create possibilities. I know not everyone loves planning as an activity, but as Sarah makes clear, it's really not optional if you want to create a calm and effective life (anyone who think it's optional probably has someone else doing their planning for them—so instead of disparaging it, how about acknowledging their hard work?). She also firmly believes that planning isn't just about tasks and have-to-dos. If you're a responsible person, you'll probably do what you have to do. Planning is about making space for what you find wonderful amid everything else. Thoughtful planning means you can get together with friends in the middle of a weekend filled with three kid sporting events and the dress rehearsal for someone else's musical. Thoughtful planning means you can make it to your book club even during a busy season at work. You might even get to watch *Dance Moms*!

I am so excited for you to read this book. Fans of Sarah's conversational voice on her podcasts will hear it sparkling on these pages, too. Who knew planning could be so entertaining? I've learned so much from Sarah. I know you will as well. You are going to emerge from reading this book with so many ideas that you might think you won't know what to do with them—but you will, because Sarah is giving you the tools to build a life you absolutely love.

Laura Vanderkam
Author, *Tranquility by Tuesday: 9 Ways to Calm the Chaos and Make Time for What Matters*,
published by Penguin Random House, 2022.
Please visit lauravanderkam.com to learn more.

Introduction

We are all on earth for a limited number of days—and an unknowable number at that. Keeping this immutable fact in mind, nothing is as precious as our time. Planning is an activity dedicated to thinking about how we'd like to allocate this nonrenewable resource, measured out in hours, days, weeks, months, and years. Logically, thinking about this time allocation deeply and with intention seems important! And yet, somehow, it's not terribly common to spend much time on planning. It's even less common to spend time *thinking* about planning practices—something I've fondly started to refer to as "meta-planning."

I very much hope this book will spawn a meta-planning revolution. And to be clear, this is not a book about stickers and washi tape (though I'm not knocking these fun planning accessories), or even choosing the perfect paper planner sidekick. It's about systems and practices and rituals, all designed to help you identify priorities, corral life's myriad inputs, and execute on the things most important to you.

Let's Start with a Tale of Two Mondays...

Monday #1

Ahh, 6:24 a.m.! You wake up to the sound of your alarm and see a text from your running friend wondering where you are—you never confirmed today's meetup, but you didn't cancel, either! You realize you will have to fit in a workout later, if at all.

You rouse the kids, frantically throw some packed lunches together, and feel mildly annoyed at yourself for not picking up the dry cleaning last week. You scowl at your limited wardrobe but put something on and head out the door. You drop the kids off at school; one kid's teacher reminds you that the box of Ronzoni pasta (IT HAS TO BE THIS BRAND! THE BRIDGE PROJECT DEMANDS PASTA UNIFORMITY!) is due tomorrow for your sixth grader's physics project—don't you remember? This was in the WhatsApp chat (buried among fourteen other messages, yes, but it was there). You resolve to pick up the pasta after work.

You head to your office and arrive right on time but without any buffer time to think through your day. Immediately, you log in to your first meeting and realize you were hoping to prep a list of questions in advance but didn't get to it; this causes the meeting to be less productive and more stressful than you envisioned. You clear out your email, putting out fires until lunch, when you are asked to start working on a project due in twenty-four hours. You say "yes" to said project without recognizing that you already have another semi-urgent request on the table, leading to a crunched afternoon. You finish with what you can and head out in time to pick up the kids from soccer practice. You arrive home to make dinner and realize you had ingredients for a slow-cooker stew, but said ingredients never actually made it into the slow cooker. You order takeout and help kids with homework and—*OH RIGHT, the Ronzoni!!!* You make a beeline to the store before closing (or beg your partner to do it in exchange for orchestrating bedtime), and you arrive back home exhausted. You crash into bed with your phone and revenge-procrastinate bedtime for an hour because you're still annoyed about the super-specific pasta and the missed workout that you're far too tired for now..

Monday #2

You wake up to your alarm—you had confirmed a meetup with your running friend last night, and you are up in time to meet her for four chatty miles. Before you head out, you consult your planner while sipping some coffee. You review your calendar and think briefly about your highest priority work tasks, writing them down on the page. This goes very quickly thanks to the more detailed planning session you conducted on Friday! In looking under the "meals" section on the weekly page, you are reminded to take out the slow cooker.

You enjoy your run, knowing the kids' lunches are already packed, so the morning launch should go relatively smoothly. You arrive home in time to get the kids up and get dressed for work in your favorite outfit. (Good thing you remembered to get it from the dry cleaner last week!) You're feeling confident with a glow from your run; you put the prepped dinner into the slow cooker you left out, set it to low, and drive the kids to school.

At drop-off, when the teacher reminds you about the Ronzoni

pasta needed for tomorrow's bridge-building extravaganza, you tell her it was no problem—you jotted it down in your planner right when you saw it on WhatsApp, so it was easy to grab with your groceries last week!

You head to your office and arrive right on time. Thankfully, you'd prepped for the week ahead on Friday, because there is a meeting right at the start of the workday! The meeting runs smoothly due to your excellent prepared questions, and you are able to capture action items to complete later with time to spare. Checking your email, you note a request for a new project due in about twenty-four hours. Reviewing your plan for the week, you note another semi-urgent project that would be due around the same time, and you ask if Wednesday would be acceptable, noting the conflict. Your colleague says yes, and you breathe a sigh of relief—it would have been hard to get both done in that time frame!

You work through the meeting's action items plus your most urgent project and end the day with a brief planning session, noting items you didn't get to and reviewing your schedule and priorities for Tuesday. Feeling a satisfying sense of closure, you enjoy your favorite podcast on the way to pick up the kids from soccer practice. You arrive home to the cozy aroma of dinner in the slow cooker, toast some pita bread to go with it, and serve it to your hungry family. You consult your planner one last time and remind your daughter to put the Ronzoni in her backpack. You spend some quality time with your partner and reflect on your day, set the coffee up for the next morning, and enjoy a night of restful sleep.

Clearly, these Monday stories are exaggerations. Even with the most tried and true processes in place, no one can plan their way out of every single life challenge that threatens a peaceful and productive existence. You might arrive home to the perfect slow-cooked meal feeling smug about your pasta preparedness only to be informed by your child that the nurse discovered lice during today's routine hair check. (Major downer, but at least you could then enjoy a decent dinner while you work on your plan to solve that dilemma!)

Still, you can shift the balance. More proactivity means less reactivity. More planning in the things you want to do means more life satisfaction and more fun. You might be holding this book because you love all things related to planning and organization, and maybe your life already resembles Monday #2. Or, you may have found your way to this page specifically because you find yourself continually frustrated by days that feel like Monday #1. Either way, welcome! I'm so glad you are here.

I believe that planning in an effective and systematic way can help almost anyone enjoy life more. This doesn't necessarily translate to getting more done in the professional sense, but it means moving through your days with direction and intention and filling our moments with things you truly want to be doing rather than reverting to various defaults.

My own personal obsession with planning began early. Currently, I am a fortysomething mother of three who tends to want to squeeze a lot out of life, and looking back, I think I always have. I have always had multiple interests and life pursuits—truthfully, often just one or two more than seemed sensible. As a teen, I was scheming to figure out how to mesh my competition cheer schedule with heavy musical involvement (violin and voice, because why pick just one?), while also doing reasonably well in school and enjoying time with friends. During college, I was on a science-heavy premed track but still wanted to sing my heart out in musicals and acapella. In medical school, I worked a side job teaching MCAT test prep and trained for marathons; I also started a blog during that busy period, oversharing on a daily basis without ever suspecting that this fun hobby would lead to multiple podcasts and my own business decades later!

All of this was perhaps preparing me for the biggest life-management challenge by far: having three children during medical training and my early medical career. Nothing compared to the logistical challenges of keeping up patient care and documentation while pumping breastmilk multiple times per day—this is perhaps when my fire was truly lit to set priorities and master task management, because there was so little room for error in my schedule, and, at the time, the stakes felt overwhelmingly high.

Currently, I see patients part time (three days per week) and spend the other two weekdays working on various creative pursuits, from podcasting to teaching others about planning to writing and beyond. I've created courses, grown my own small business, and generated a hybrid career without following any path I had seen before. I still exercise almost every day (in my pilates and strength era!), read regularly, spend one-on-one time with each of my kids, and enjoy quality time with my husband. We take great family trips and enjoy downtime and rest, too—there are few things I love more than a Saturday afternoon nap on the couch. I feel lucky to get to do quite a lot, and I think I pack a lot of joy into my days. I handle many tasks (as do we all!), but I don't find managing things to be stressful or onerous...most of the time.

At various junctures of my life, I've noticed raised eyebrows wondering if what I had on my plate was realistic or if instead I would crash and burn. Sometimes I have had to make hard choices, but for the most part I have been able to continue doing a healthy number of things that bring me joy. I recognize that some of this success may be attributed to pure luck, plus various forms of privilege and support. But another common thread laced through these years has been a persistent dedication to planning—considerable energy and plenty of time devoted to thinking through my priorities and how I want to allocate my limited hours.

For decades now, I have enjoyed planning in multiple formats and using various techniques, starting with random Hallmark store journals in my teens to paper planners in my college years and digital/paper hybrid methods in my twenties and beyond. Over time, I have experimented with my own techniques, read and learned from many time-management experts, and gradually come to understand the most important elements of planning for every life season.

Fast-forward to the present, and my passion for planning has only grown stronger. With my own systems down, in recent years I've put more focus on learning what works for and resonates with others. I have honed the methods shared in this book even further through years of speaking and teaching, from the lessons shared in my podcast *Best Laid Plans* (over two hundred episodes in!) to the multiple rounds of live instruction I have delivered effectively through a course

I developed called Best Laid Plans Academy. Academy participants and podcast listeners have frequently shared with me their success stories, which often culminate in an amazing achievement, accompanied by a profound feeling of peace that they did not have before they put these structured practices into play. It has been incredibly rewarding to be a part of their journeys, and I hope that this book serves to bring these lessons to a wider audience. Notably, I also believe that this book's perspective truly stands out in the personal-development canon, which is dominated by "productivity bros" with entirely flexible schedules and, behind the scenes, wives (or partners) managing life's minutia for them. These days, I do have *some* flexibility (which is good, because otherwise you would not be reading this!), but I also know what it is like to work full time and then some in a not-so-flexible role. Like my colleagues, I still take call seven days and nights at a stretch multiple times per year, which means being available for any urgent clinical situation in my field that arises. I rely heavily on my own planning tools and systems to help me through these challenging weeks!

It's not just me. By nature, most humans love to strive and make progress on things that feel important. If you're reading this, I would guess you're probably doing plenty of this and likely in multiple realms of life. Everyone wants to achieve some kind of dream, whether it involves career aspirations, a personal goal, family life ideals, or a combination of all of the above. However, many people feel overwhelmed by the constant barrage of obligations that seem to come at them from every angle. Women especially face challenges as they commonly attempt to carry the mental load of the household in addition to their personal and professional pursuits. Too often, this sense of overwhelm leads people into routines that do not serve them or life paths that remain on autopilot. Trying to navigate this complex landscape without airtight systems for managing the multitude of inputs and an effective method for keeping track of one's goals can be incredibly frustrating, leading to a sense of futility and hopelessness.

What if instead of greeting each day with confusion about the day's priorities and schedule, you had a clearly laid out plan, complete with breathing room for rest and time for fun? Imagine a day where instead of reacting to stimuli every few minutes, you were able to proactively make incremental progress toward your core goals, both personal and professional. Imagine no longer dreading Mondays, but instead entering into the workweek feeling confident that your curated calendar reflects reality and that your task list is current, realistic, and designed to help you move forward in the ways that support their true priorities. And finally, imagine ultimately realizing those previously mentioned dreams by moving and iterating incrementally toward the career or life that you always wanted, with room for some discovery and even serendipity along the way.

All of this is possible with the right systems in place, yet you may not have spent much time optimizing your planning methods and tools, since this just isn't commonly discussed or taught in schools. I very much hope you will feel like a confident planner change after absorbing the methods and practices within this book. Let the following chapters serve as your comprehensive guide to help you craft your own custom systems and life-management structures at every level, from daily planning to long-term visioning. You will learn airtight task-capture and time management methods to prevent death from a thousand cuts due to requests coming from every direction. No one can ever shift life entirely away from reactivity, but you will find yourself shifting the balance into the proactive realm more often, and there will be backup systems and ideas for when things get challenging—around travel, life stress, mental-health struggles, and more.

I believe this book and its methods have the power to be life-changing to the many people who are currently feeling adrift in a sea of never-ending tasks and goals that get thrown out into the universe early in the year only to be forgotten by March. The work will be structured similarly to the coursework I have taught multiple times in Best Laid Plans Academy, opening with broad strokes planning and life-management essentials and then guiding you through effective planning techniques at every time horizon, from annual all the way to daily. With a bit of practice and customization, you will become confident in these methods and achieve greater clarity in your goals so you can make the most out your life while enjoying more peace and having more fun along the way.

Essential Tools

One Master Calendar, Nested Goals, and Airtight Task Capture

One of the most common questions I receive is a version of this: "I have a very busy life, managing work, kids, and more! I never feel like I know what I should be doing next, and I am ready to get organized. *Which planner should I use?*"

Sometimes, desperation to find the right methods even leads to a reckless planner shopping spree. I've seen some cases of planner wanderlust that are pretty severe: stacks of planners six books high, plus five different apps promising to help with habit tracking, task capture, photo organization, and so much more! But instead of helping the situation, the once-eager buyer just ends up more confused, and now it takes ten minutes to even figure out which book or app contains the most current schedule. The mistake here is that even with the best of intentions, this person is focusing on the products rather than the essential processes. It's not his or her fault there's tons of marketing around planners and tools and far less discussion around how to actually use them effectively!

I love the idea that a perfect planner or digital planning tool could be an easy bridge to a less reactive existence. But while I adore beautiful planning tools and well-designed apps, I do not believe that either provides the key to an organized and intentional life. For better or worse, your life-management needs are greater and more complex than anything an aesthetically pleasing daily tracking page or monthly layout can offer. It is the planning practices and techniques that truly matter, not the products used. A complete and effective system is what makes all the difference. In this chapter, I want to introduce you to the three most important planning concepts and techniques that we'll be using as we move through the book.

Over the course of working with many people searching for planner peace, I have identified three elements at the core of every efficient and effective setup. There will be plenty of detail to follow, but let's start with an overview of these three keys:.

1. **A functional calendar system** that includes everything you have actually committed to do at a specific time collected in one very reliable place, hereafter referred to as your **master calendar**. This can be entirely paper-based or completely digital, but the nonnegotiable aspects are its completeness and accuracy.

2. **An effective goal-setting system** that allows for goals to stay top of mind and also be scaled effectively to each time frame. The system I use will be described in detail in this chapter; it involves setting goals at the annual, seasonal, monthly, weekly, and daily levels. I

coined the term **nested goal setting** to reflect the way each level's goals stem from the time horizon above.

3. **A comprehensive task and input management system** that ensures you are handling life's various inputs at the right cadence without losing anything of importance. In order to shift the balance in your life away from reactivity, you need to feel confident that you know what is on your plate at any given moment and that you have a proven method for processing new tasks or information as they arise. **Airtight task management** is the goal, and in this chapter you will learn routines and processes around managing your inputs to help achieve this.

If you have these three things mastered and optimized, the specific tools truly do not matter. You could plan in a ninety-nine-cent Mead notebook and have better results than someone who has a planner stack ten volumes high or subscribes to the twelve hottest productivity apps on the market! This chapter will include my favorite approaches to each of these planning essentials, and by the end you will be set up for planning success and ready to plan at every time horizon from yearly to daily.

Your Master Calendar: A Source You Can Trust

Keeping an accurate calendar seems basic, and yet I have seen this become more of a struggle in recent years, in spite of—or perhaps because of—the proliferation of digital calendaring and time-management tools. Many people keep their home calendar in one place (on the fridge, perhaps), their work calendar in another (Outlook or another work-mandated tool), and random events shared on digital calendars native to their devices. Oh, and there's that soccer game app and the school calendar system and none of these can be shared with your work calendar, because that's a closed system and contains private information. As a result, you might find yourself heading into each week resigned to the fact that there will probably be surprises…and not the fun kind.

Sound appealing? I didn't think so.

To avoid the mess that ensues when calendars have gaps and don't communicate, you need two things: (1) an awareness of where all of the incomplete calendars are and (2) one regularly updated master calendar. The idea of one master calendar to rule them all captures the reality that many are reluctant to acknowledge: having multiple time-specific items strewn about different systems is a productivity nightmare. There is no quicker route to reactivity than an event or time-sensitive task that sneaks up on you at the last minute or even after the fact!

To ensure your master calendar is kept up-to-date with everything so that it can live up to its name, it is essential to develop a clear understanding of where all of the relevant calendars are. That way, you can ensure that they either auto-integrate with your master calendar (example: ensuring that data from the soccer app regularly feeds into your Google Calendar, if that's what you use) or that you have a manual system in place for syncing up relevant dates (example: writing all of the no-school days into your paper planner).

I recommend creating a table such as the one here to list out each of your various calendars and describe how each will make its way into your master calendar.

TYPE OF CALENDAR	WHERE IT IS FOUND	HOW IT INTEGRATES
Example 1: Soccer practices and games	GotSports app	Automatically pulls to electronic calendar
Example 2: School calendar and events	Emailed, plus PDF from beginning of school year	Manually—must plug dates into calendar

The second piece to maintaining your master calendar is to be ruthless about consulting it before committing to anything and then immediately entering in commitments as they are decided upon. If your master calendar is a paper planner, you will need to bring it to the dentist if you plan on making your next appointment while you are there. (Worst case, if you don't have it, you can make a tentative appointment, but immediately email or text yourself a note or create a timed reminder to consult your planner and reschedule if needed as soon as you are around your planner.) If you have committed to doing *anything* time specific, whether it is a key work meeting, carpool pickup, or a morning workout class, it belongs on your master calendar. This will help eliminate conflicts and create a reliable place to look for your level of busyness as you choose your tasks or goals list for the day (or week, or month—more on that to come).

Calendars You May Have

- Personal schedule (appointments, events)
- Work schedule
- School calendars
- Sports team or activity calendars
- Fitness schedule
- Meal-planning calendar
- Community calendar (events, trash pickup days)
- Religious calendar

Some people prefer to keep separate work and life calendars. I generally advise against this, but sometimes there are confidentiality issues that necessitate a guardrail. If this is the case, I recommend you put a very nonspecific item such as "WORK" into your master calendar to span the hours you are at work, and then you can use your work-specific tool at work. Admittedly, I do something like this myself. Since I see patients some days and definitely cannot include patient data in my planner, I'll just write "Patients" in each four-hour clinic block. While actively seeing patients, I'm essentially following the schedule laid out for me on our electronic health record. However, any work commitment outside of these blocks would be entered into my master calendar separately. An attorney might do something similar, but it would be important to note in the master calendar if there are any work-related meetings or events that happen outside of designated or typical work blocks. The specific names and any confidential information should be left off, of course, but it would still be helpful to know that on Tuesday at 6:00 p.m. you have an important after-hours call.

Sometimes you may find that an awareness of *others'* calendars can become important, and in this case, including the relevant details in your own master calendar can be helpful. For example, my week will look and feel very different if my kids are away at a weeklong camp or if my husband is traveling for work. In general, if I am responsible for driving or if I know it may impact the flow of my day in some way, I include my kids' activities on my master calendar. Things do get crowded on occasion, but I've been able to find layouts that work for me even on paper, and digital calendars can be viewed in layers that can be toggled on and off for more clarity when needed.

Since different views and layouts work for different styles of thinking, I keep an open mind when it comes to tools and generally try to avoid being overly prescriptive. That said, I do think a weekly vertical layout with hourly markings is the easiest way to visualize a week at a time. This view is popular on commonly used digital calendars, and it can be found in many popular paper planners as well. If you love to plan on paper, I personally love the versatility of the spread in the Hobonichi Cousin planner (a planner I've come back to year after year!), but there is a huge array of great options to choose from, so you can pick your favorite paper type and aesthetic.

Nested Goal Setting

It is incredibly common to generate a list of goals. January 1 is a motivator for many; often people will be inspired to create a list of very big goals in multiple areas of life. I absolutely love reading these lists! Every January, I devour podcast episodes and blog posts devoted to other people's annual goals lists, because I find them fascinating and inspiring.

Smaller- scale goals lists are common, too. Even the popular "brain dump" is often a goals list of sorts, comprised of things on your mind that are nagging you to either schedule or get done within a certain time frame. A daily to-do list can also be a goals list, even if the word "goals" sounds a bit loftier in scope than items like "order cat food" or "schedule car maintenance."

These lists can be useful and really do stem from a hopeful and positive place! However, the problem that arises with these lists is that they can so easily become lost and forgotten in the whirlwind of life. What happens to those annual goals lists in March? What happens to the items on your brain dump list that didn't get finished or captured in some other form? Missing from simple list-making methodology is some kind of connection between the lists, a way of carrying tasks forward from year to season to month to week to day, where real progress can be made.

Enter the nested goals method. With nested goals, you create a goals list at every time horizon, beginning with annual. (Note: there is a step-by-step guide to this process in the next chapter, so if this sounds daunting, don't worry!) Then, as you approach each lower-level time frame, you create that list while consulting the list from the time horizon above it. In addition to your higher-level lists, you also think about upcoming priorities and the time you have available. That's it, in a nutshell—and it works at every level down to daily planning.

This sounds complex but actually becomes quite intuitive in practice. On the next page are examples demonstrating how this works at each time horizon below annual.

Understanding Nested Goals

Annually
List out your annual goals.

JAN | FEB | MAR | APR | MAY | JUN | JUL | AUG | SEPT | OCT | NOV | DEC

Seasonally
Seasonal goals are generated by integrating annual goals with current happenings within the season

Q1 Q2 Q3 Q4

Monthly
Monthly goals are inspired by referencing seasonal goals and adding priorities that apply to the upcoming month.

JAN FEB MAR APR MAY JUN JUL AUG SEPT OCT NOV DEC

Weekly
Goals often become tasks at this level, integrating items from the monthly list and considering the week's calendar landscape

WEEK 1 WEEK 2 WEEK 3 WEEK 4

Daily
Daily tasks are selected with review of your weekly list, plus careful consideration of the day's schedule, your current priorities, and how you feel

M T W TH F SA SU

Example 1: Seasonal goal setting

Let's say it's almost summer, and you are conducting your seasonal planning session on a free afternoon in late May (much more on that in chapter 3). In order to create a list of goals for the upcoming season of summer, you will consult your previous seasonal list (in this case, your Spring list) plus your annual list. Reviewing your previous list will help you to identify items to carry forward, if they still feel relevant, and your annual list will continue to remind you of the goals that felt important to you—things you really felt would make it a great year.

You will also consider upcoming events (consulting your master calendar) and reflect in a more general sense on how you are feeling this season. This might include assessment of your energy levels, your health status, your stress levels, and what you are feeling enthusiastic about. Integrating your longer-term annual vision with this season's demands and your current reality will help you create a realistic and effective seasonal list for your summer.

Example 2: Monthly goal setting

You've reached the end of June and are starting to think about the month ahead. As part of your monthly review session (more details in chapter 4), you bring out your June monthly list and also consult your seasonal (Summer) goals list. You take a moment to celebrate two wins already achieved on your June list, and then decide what, if anything, to carry forward to July. You consult the calendar landscape up ahead, which is probably fairly detailed at this point as you are scanning a four-week time frame, and you assess your overall energy levels. Just as in the seasonal example, you can then factor in all of the above and generate a July list that fits your energy, addresses time-sensitive matters, and incorporates elements that move you toward your larger vision.

Example 3: Weekly goal setting

The specifics of your weekly review process will be discussed in chapter 5, but one of the essential elements is your weekly goal setting. The nested method still applies! Just like in the broader time horizons, you will first consult your prior weekly goals list and your monthly list. At this point, the "goals" on your lists may start to sound simpler or more like tasks. That's okay, and, in fact, it is very much appropriate with a smaller time frame! The semantics don't matter; whatever you'd like to call them, the items on your list are *things you'd like to get done*, and most larger-scale goals are really just collections of small tasks linked together and/or repeated over time, anyway.

Just like the levels above, before committing to your weekly goals, you will consider your calendar (which is likely fairly well-defined at this level), your energy, and generally what is going on around you. You wouldn't want to assign yourself a meaty work task while you're recovering from the flu, and you might want to scale back on tasks that aren't time sensitive if you have a big project due. By considering these factors, you will be able to generate a list that is realistic and motivating rather than demoralizing.

Example 4: Daily goal setting

It's Wednesday morning! You sit down at your desk to plan your day (more on this in chapter 6), and as part of your routine you create a goals list for the day. In this case, the items are probably going to be largely one-step tasks, so today's list could be also accurately referred to as your task list or to- do list.

Again, as in the levels above, you'll consult two lists during this brief planning session: your list from yesterday and your list for the week. You will then pull out your master calendar. At this zoomed-in level, you likely have specific ideas as to where you need to be and when and what is time sensitive; you will use this information to inform your day's list. Sometimes, a calendar item within that day will generate its own associated task, such as when you need to do some preparation just before a meeting.

Finally, just like with the other levels, you will also consider your holistic sense of what kind of day it is. If you are attempting to work from home with a sick kid, you will probably need to keep your list as short as possible (and you might have to add some items related to said kid to your list, such as making a doctor's appointment or running out to get medication). This assessment step will prevent you from overloading yourself on a day when you really don't feel up to it. This will help you to trust your lists and will lead to a greater sense of overall peace and confidence in your system.

The nested goals system sounds like a lot of lists because it *is* a lot of lists: to be exact, 435 per year if you're planning with five seasons. (Yes, you read that right—you can plan with five seasons, if it best fits your life rhythms! I'll share more about quintile planning in chapter 3.) But a year is quite a lot of time, and generating these lists becomes more and more efficient as you master this practice. Often, a thoughtful and realistic daily list can be generated in under ten minutes. The larger-scale lists take a bit longer, but assuming thirty minutes for your weekly list and an hour (likely an overestimate) for monthly and above, this would add up to just over one hundred hours for the entire year, or 1.7 percent of your waking hours assuming eight hours of sleep.

Spending 1.7 percent of your waking hours to plan the other 98.3 percent seems like a worthwhile investment from my perspective, but if even that seems like too much, you can scale things down and still have a functional system. Some people may choose not to create a fresh list for every day; this may be particularly appropriate for those with very fixed schedules (example: a physician with scheduled appointments). Some might prefer to make just one list for the weekend, and I personally don't tend to make any lists when I'm on vacation with family! Others may choose to skip the monthly level altogether, going straight from seasonal to weekly. This system is flexible and forgiving; you can pick up where you left off if you miss a season or two.

That said, the nested goals system truly shines when you are reasonably consistent. By reviewing your annual list every time you create your seasonal list, you are guaranteed to see it every season (three to five times per year, depending on how you prefer to divide your year). You will not forget about those annual goals you spent time and energy generating in January because you will see them at relatively regular intervals throughout the entire year. The same holds true for seasonal goals; that summer list won't be buried at the bottom of your beach bag come August, because you'll be pulling it out as that month rolls around.

At the same time, having designated times to pull out these higher-level lists means that you can avoid thinking about them when you don't need to, which can be a source of stress and wasted mental energy. In fact, one of the reasons I developed this system is because I found the idea of being confronted with a wide array of options every day incredibly overwhelming and almost paralyzing at times. If you follow time-management expert David Allen, you might be familiar with his method of creating context-based lists,[1] which are organized by the place where you are most likely to do them. These lists are incredibly comprehensive, essentially containing everything you want to do that is not relegated to a more nebulous "someday" category. This can mean hundreds of items corralled together, and with our digital tools capable of storing almost limitless pieces of data, you can create a sense of task overload very quickly and easily.

In contrast, with the nested goals method, most days you are only looking at your list for the week and the day. Because these lists are informed by higher-level lists, you won't lose momentum toward your biggest priorities, but you will be able to see only what you need to see to have a successful day, avoiding the sense of overwhelm that can bubble up when we spend too much time thinking about what we're not accomplishing.

Commonly, I get asked where these lists should live. There is no right answer or one perfect place to store these lists, but the chosen tool must be something that (a) you will not lose and (b) that you enjoy using. You can also use different tools at different levels, and sometimes a little bit of digital/analog redundancy can be helpful!

I personally prefer to write out my goals by hand, because I enjoy it and there is something about the act of writing things out that tends to slow me down (in a good way!) and bring out my more reflective side. At the same time, I am practical and want to be able to access my higher-level goals (yearly and seasonal) on the go, when I may not have my planner with me. Therefore, I tend to handwrite these goals on blank pages in a yearly planner, but I also take a picture of these goals for posterity and save them in my electronic brain (more on that later). My monthly goals also go in my planner (often beside the monthly calendar, or on a blank page if the planner I am using has one for each month), and so do my weekly and daily lists.

That said, these lists could also be entirely digital. You could put all of your lists for the year in a set of (nested!) folders in an app like Notion or Apple Notes, or you could use a more goal-specific app like Todoist to create lists for each time frame. The tools are going to shift with time and what is trending, but the methods work regardless of the specific tools selected, so use the tool you enjoy the most!

Some users find it very helpful to have older lists to refer back to year after year, as this might help them come up with recurring items that seem unexpected but aren't, like camp signups in February. Others prefer starting with a blank slate every year. The specifics of where are not important, but a system that is easy to use and brings you joy will keep you coming back week after week, season after season.

Airtight Task Management

In his iconic 2001 time-management manual *Getting Things Done*, David Allen stated wisely: "Your mind is for having ideas, not for holding them."[2] At the time, he could have only imagined the current pace at which most of us now receive ideas, assignments, alerts, reminders, and other communications through our devices—all of which could be classified as inputs and all of which need to be somehow tracked and managed. If our brains felt bogged down then, you can only imagine how much more difficult things are today.

Airtight task management can be challenging, but it is worthwhile for many. So many of us are living with the residue of incomplete tasks, due dates, and demands just floating around in our minds, perhaps even in our subconscious. This phenomenon is well known enough to have a name: the Zeigarnik effect, named after a Russian psychologist who noted that waitstaff in a restaurant had a much easier time remembering the orders of patrons who hadn't yet paid.[3] The task felt incomplete (David Allen refers to this quite aptly as an "open loop"), and so it nagged at them until it was done.

From an evolutionary perspective, it's easy to imagine why this phenomenon would be in place. But with the number of pieces of information coming at us rapid-fire in today's world, the effect could go from useful to terribly burdensome. Just thinking about an overstuffed email inbox, there could be the equivalent of hundreds of unfilled and unpaid orders in there. Open loops galore!

It is enough to drag us down, and in many cases it does, leading to procrastination or just a general sense of unease or distraction. On the flip side, if we know we have a foolproof system for capturing the myriad inputs that are thrown at us, we can be more relaxed about them. We can be confident that all of these open loops can and will be processed in time, leaving us more efficient and clearheaded in the long run—and more likely to actually get the things that feel important to us done.

So how do we capture and corral all of these inputs? As is the case with goal setting and calendar management, you need a thoughtful system! The first step in setting one up is to make a master list of all of your inboxes. Some of these will be obvious: your work email; your personal email; your physical mailbox. Some will be sneakier; perhaps your kids' soccer coach loves to put vital information in a WhatsApp thread or sports-specific app. Some will be virtual (apps, email, inter-office messaging, and electronic health record inboxes are some examples) and some will be physical (the mail, stacks of paper that accumulate in your office, or your first grader's backpack!).

Once you have your list, make an intentional decision about how often you will process each inbox. There is no one right answer to how often you need to process your email, but an attempt at somewhat regular processing is going to serve you far better than no system at all.

Note that I said "processing," not necessarily emptying. I personally do love an empty inbox and encourage course participants to at least try getting to Inbox Zero once so they can see what is like. Side note: invariably, someone will note that they have 75,000 emails and wonder how in the world clearing out that box would even be possible without dedicating weeks to email alone. To counter, if you have 75,000 emails, you probably aren't seeing 74,900 of them very often. I don't necessarily recommend deleting a packed inbox, but in many cases you can at least do some kind of bulk archive to acknowledge the reality that pages ten through five hundred of your inbox probably aren't being looked at anyway! In the age of pretty decent search engines and relatively affordable storage, you can do a mass archive and limit your processing to maybe ~ten screens full of email—the last five hundred or so.

Once you have your list of inboxes, you need to clarify when and where you will process them. Choosing your cadence of processing intervals can be challenging, as you want to pick time frames that won't cause you to miss much of importance yet are long enough so that you can avoid compulsively checking continuously throughout your day! This can be a fine line, so be prepared to adjust. It goes without saying that different inboxes are going to have different cadences; your urgent work messages are going to be dealt with frequently and your physical mail might be dealt with weekly.

Take the time to think through what makes sense for each of your inboxes, and also think about when these processing sessions will occur. Like it or not, this administrative work takes time and effort. Many people find that a weekly email processing block is something that deserves its own dedicated calendar slot, and not necessarily a short one! This doesn't mean you won't do ongoing triage to see if there are any metaphorical fires to put out, but you can feel confident knowing the nonurgent things will be dealt with, organized, and not lost. And while the processing itself isn't exactly a party, you will likely feel great after your weekly (or biweekly or daily) processing session knowing exactly what you have on your plate.

Processing is a bit of a vague term I've been using, so let's clarify what this means. For each message or physical input item (such as a piece of mail or paper on your desk), ask yourself the following questions:

1. Is this a task to assign myself?

2. Does this message represent a calendar item I need to note somewhere?

3. Is this a piece of information I will need to see at a specific time (i.e., on a trip, or just before a meeting)?

4. Is this item something that is not time specific but that feels important enough to store outside of just archiving it?

5. Do I need to take time to write a detailed response?

If none of the above apply, the message or input is probably spam or junk mail and can be deleted (or archived, if we're talking about a digital inbox, or if you are not short on space, and you want it to be searchable on the off chance it becomes relevant someday). For the rest of the categories, let's discuss processing in more detail.

Category 1: Tasks

Many inboxes are filled with tasks. Some of these are specific assignments for you (prepare slide deck for upcoming meeting; purchase cupcakes for bake sale). Some are tasks to be delegated to others. If an item contains a task for you to do (and you are agreeing to do it), add it to the time-frame-specific list that feels most appropriate or assign it to a specific day.

For me, it works well to use the same time horizons for sorting tasks as we discussed in the nested goal setting section (page 19). As discussed previously, as you zoom in past the monthly level, goals lists often morph into task lists, anyway. You can use your paper or digital planning app of choice (or a separate task-management app, if you prefer) to create a list for each day, week, month, season, and year. I'm not suggesting anyone build an unwieldy system of four hundred lists; this can be as simple as adding your task to your planner's weekly view or generating a day-specific task in your digital calendar.

If your task is very time specific, assign it to a specific day or schedule a specific time to do it in your calendar. If it's more of a "need to do soon, but not at any specific point" kind of assignment, place it on a weekly list. If my current week is jam packed, I'll often scan ahead in my planner for a week with more white space and record the task there.

If it's something you're hoping to consider for an upcoming season, add it to wherever you do your seasonal lists. There is no shame in having some holiday ideas captured over the summer! Finally, if the task has no clear time frame and in fact you don't see yourself addressing it this year, you will add it to your someday possibilities list.

My someday possibilities list idea stems from David Allen's concept of "someday/maybe," a list where he recommends parking anything that is up for consideration

Someday Possibilities Examples

Here are a few items from my someday possibilities list—all ideas I want to keep around because I don't want to forget about them, but I have no plans to execute on in any specific short-term time frame.

- Go on a writing retreat.
- Publish article about organizing tips for physicians.
- Workshop at endocrine meeting.
- Get an organizing certification.
- Go to Japan for the Hobonichi launch.
- Write a medical memoir (with some notes for chapter ideas).
- Do an "Open That Bottle Night" party.

in the future but not happening now. I don't necessarily think every single idea you generate needs to go on that list, as lists with hundreds of items cease to be all that helpful. Reserve this list for things that truly do feel important to you but just can't happen right now. The idea for this book sat on my own someday possibilities list for many years only to be moved ceremoniously onto an annual goals list when the time was right.

By capturing every task in this manner, you are far less likely to miss a signup deadline or be surprised by an urgent need that could have been addressed much more easily in advance.

Of note, some tasks will be very small and obvious. For those tasks that you know are entirely straightforward and quick, you can choose to do them immediately rather than recording them anywhere. You do have to be careful here, as some things that seem easy can become less so very quickly ("rent car" sounds fast but might lead you down a rabbit hole of deal-searching and logistics analysis). For me, tasks that fit into the "just do it" category include things like recording an expense, doing a quick bill payment online, or ordering something specific quickly from an online retailer.

Category 2: Calendar Items

At certain times of year, a decent chunk of your inputs from various channels may be calendar items in (flimsy) disguise! These might include emails announcing an important work conference, a new recurring meeting, or your child's gymnastics meet schedule. As you process your inbox, these items are easy; you just have to move the information out of your inbox and into your actual calendar, ideally your master calendar. I always have my planner right by my side as I process email, both to assign myself tasks and to add calendar items. If your calendar is digital and you don't have a double-screen setup, you can use your phone (or another device) to enter calendar items while doing your processing so that you can avoid inefficient swapping between multiple tabs and windows.

Category 3: Time- or Context-Specific Information

Another common category of inputs is that of time- or context-specific information. These are pieces of information that are currently sitting in an inbox, but you know you'll need to reference them later at a specific moment or in a given situation, like a school form that will need to be filled out at your child's next doctor's appointment. For these kinds of items, it's best to move them to a place where you know you'll be able to find them at the moment of need.

If the material is time specific, you can attach it directly to your digital calendar entry in many calendar apps. If you plan on paper, you can simply leave yourself a note as to where you can find the info, if it won't be obvious. Many things can then just be archived, if you know you'll be able to access email on a given date.

If the material is context-specific and you want to make it easy to find, you need some kind of digital (or perhaps even physical, but I find digital much easier—and searchable!) filing system. There are many ways to set one up, but I found a lot of value in Tiago Forte's methods outlined in *Building a Second Brain.*[4] He recommends using a digital notes app and setting up folders in four categories: projects, areas of life (I include work, kids, and travel, among others), reference, and archives. Each of these categories can have as many subcategories as you want, essentially creating a flexible and searchable digital filing cabinet. Creating an organized digital system for things you really want to able to access easily later can be incredibly helpful, and it's a perfect place to save items that feel a bit too salient to exist only in your email archives.

As a personal example, I tend to do most of our family travel planning. Whenever I receive an email confirmation related to an upcoming trip, I take a quick screenshot and add it to a trip-specific subfolder within the "Travel" folder of my second brain, which happens to be in Apple Notes. This way, I can quickly pull up any travel-related document even without relying on cellular data or a Wifi signal, and all of the info is organized in one place. Once I've saved it in this manner, I archive the email. This leaves my inbox clear and the information easily accessible.

Category 4: Things That Are Not Time Specific but Feel Important

Sometimes you will have items a bit like those in the previous category, but the way you will want to see them in the future feels more uncertain. An example might be a camp program that looks interesting, but sign-ups are months away and you are not even sure if your child would be interested. In this case, you could put some kind of reminder about the idea in your calendar on a future date, perhaps a week before signups actually open. Or you could park this idea on your upcoming seasonal list to mull over in the future. It may not become reality, but at least you've pinged your future self to give it consideration.

If the item is truly vague in scope, you could save it on your someday possibilities list. That way, you'll at least see it when you review that list, ideally on a seasonal basis (more on that to come!).

Category 5: Items Requiring Action or a Detailed Response

Yes, in a crowded inbox (or paper pile) there are always some items that require thought and time! This tends to be the most time- and energy-consuming part of processing any inbox, and I typically save all of these for last. This is possibly part avoidance, but it also feels more manageable to tackle, say, thirty messages that require response when they are not buried alongside four hundred others. Plus, sometimes in processing the rest of your messages or inputs, you glean information that actually makes responding a bit easier or even unnecessary!

The number and scope of messages requiring response is going to vary from person to person, but after processing your inboxes a few times you will start to know how long this is likely to take, and you will build it into your week. Then, how you tackle those messages is up to you, but I like to go straight from the top and charge through, perhaps taking a break at the halfway point. You will quickly learn what processing cadence works for you and how long a buildup of about a week's time will take to clear.

Now, you have conquered your various inboxes! But there still may be things that are tossed at you when you least expect it. Perhaps your child's classmate asks you about a meetup when you are walking toward the school. Rather than trying to force yourself to remember the dates proposed, you need some kind of on-the-fly capture method that you know you will process appropriately. I tend to rely on either texting myself (yes, you can do that—just leave it unread so it doesn't get lost!) or emailing myself. Others may prefer a small paper notebook that gets processed every day. The important piece is to capture the information in a format where you know you will see it later and can then put it into your real system, whether that is paper, digital, or a mix of both.

Taken together, this chapter includes a powerhouse trifecta of planning essentials: calendar management strategies (master calendar), a goal-setting system (nested goals), and a way to manage the deluge of inputs you see every day (airtight task management). You'll be using these tools throughout the rest of the book as we discuss planning at every time horizon, so don't worry if it sounds like a lot at the outset. The idea is not to have everything set up perfectly all at once but to build and iterate over time to create a system that really works for you.

In the next chapter, you'll start to put these essential tools to use as you begin your planning journey at the broadest time horizon we'll be working with: the year!

Annual Planning

With your essential planning systems in place, the first time horizon to focus on is the broadest one: the year ahead, filled with the most uncertainty and potential.

The year as a time frame can be deceptive. Three hundred and sixty-five days sounds incredibly expansive in the abstract; it may seem like enough time for almost anything! And that is probably true, but at the same time, a year will not contain enough time for *everything*. You will want to give yourself leeway to dream and reflect freely on what you want out of the year, but you will also need to cull that list into a workable size and state.

If we all had unlimited time, planning probably wouldn't be all that important. But we don't have unlimited time, so thinking about what you can realistically accomplish and experience in your next year of life is essential. In order to do this right, you will need time and space to do careful planning; for many, this process takes up a full day or two. You will need some structure to this longer planning session, and you will need to be in the right frame of mind to really focus on your true priorities. But before getting into logistics, I hope to convince you of the value and reasoning behind investing your time, energy, and resources into your yearly planning.

Why Plan Annually?

Not everyone likes setting goals (or resolutions) for the new year. But there is a collective energy toward this frame of mind at several points throughout the year! This varies by culture—in Japan, the ultimate fresh start is in the spring, with planners often starting on April 1. American academic calendars commonly kick off in August. Residency training famously begins on July 1—perhaps a time to avoid getting that elective procedure.

The ultimate fresh-start date for many remains January 1, and January often provides many goal setters with a spark that is scarce during the other eleven months of the year. Creating a list of resolutions certainly isn't a guarantee that anything long term will take place, but it often feels appropriate to take stock and do some formalized goal generation when it's just part of the cultural fabric. While you can choose any time of year for your fresh start, why not take advantage of this extra bit of momentum?

A year is a very useful interval. As noted previously, it can be tricky—sometimes people feel like a year is everlasting, when it is decidedly finite. But 365 days is still a good number of days! You can accomplish a lot within a span of twelve months, especially if you continue to push forward on your goals past February.

Examples of projects that could realistically happen within a one-year time frame:

- Remodeling a home
- Obtaining a professional certification
- Supporting your child through a school transition
- Starting a small business
- Training for and running a marathon

These are big goals, and achieving feats of this scope can make a big difference in a person's life. A year is enough time to make progress on projects that contain multiple time-consuming steps, yet it's not such a wide span of time that it's hard to imagine what your life will look like at the end. In fact, if someone were to define a span of time most useful for planning out and thinking though Life's Big Things, they may well come up with something close to a year.

Taken together, we have an interval that is easily defined but is still a meaningfully large chunk of life, one where good-sized dreams can become reality in many cases, plus you have cultural forces at play pushing you toward goal setting and making a fresh start. Why *wouldn't* you take advantage of this perfect planning setup? Here we go—let's get started!

Your Annual Planning Retreat

Retreats are definitely trending these days. There are meditation retreats, reading retreats, sports-focused retreats, and more. Planning retreats certainly have a place in the business world, often called something like "Strategic Planning Summit" or "Company Vision Retreat." There is no reason why this concept has to stay in the business realm, though! An annual planning retreat can be had by all, in whatever format works best.

One version of this retreat could take the shape of a more traditional business conference. I didn't see where this existed in the market for individuals, so I decided to launch one on my own in 2023. Best Laid Plans: Planning 2024 took place in Fort Lauderdale, with twenty women joining me for a weekend of planning and relaxing in the Florida sun. Many of the participants loved the getaway aspects of this event, especially those who had young kids at home. They needed the physical space and emotional distance from their fast-paced everyday lives to be able to think deeply about their desires for the year ahead. There were major social benefits, too! Participants were able to compare notes, troubleshoot aspects of things they may have struggled with in the past, and generally felt able to focus on planning when everyone around them was doing the same thing.

I am mentioning this not to convince everyone reading this to attend one of my future retreats—though of course, you are all invited! —but rather because I think there are elements of this experience that are applicable to all, whether you are able to travel or tied to your home base for the time being.

Logistical Recommendations for Your Annual Planning Retreat

1. **Give yourself enough time and space.** I recommend at least one full day of planning, ideally away from everyday life

interruptions. There are many ways you can approach this! You could check yourself into a local hotel for one night. You could take a day of paid leave on a weekday and hunker down in various community locations (perhaps a local garden with tables in the morning and a library or bookstore in the afternoon). You could block off four consecutive Friday afternoons in December (maybe Fridays aren't the most productive, anyway?) and close your office door to intruders. Or you could split a weekend with your partner—one person gets a free Saturday away from kids and household responsibilities, and the other gets Sunday. Whatever structure works for you, the important parts are that your time is protected and that you have some structure to your session.

2. **Consider planning with others.** I will admit my husband is not a natural planner. However, several years ago I discovered that if we are both relaxed enough, time together spent planning is not only incredibly useful, but also kind of fun. Annual planning can be done in pairs or groups, whether you choose to partner up with your actual life partner, a friend, a family member, or a group of like-minded planning aficionados at a conference. It may be helpful to structure part of your retreat together even if you do your own solo brainstorming and visioning.

   This is of particular importance if your plans are going to involve others. I wouldn't want our family's vacations to be set without my input, and I'm pretty sure my husband feels the same way! Even plans that don't involve everyone quite as directly can have impact across a household (Example: deciding to train for a marathon). It is nice to have other stakeholders involved as you set your big intentions, and ideally you will then be able to support each other throughout the year as your dreams unfold.

3. **Mark this in your calendar!** Half the battle in making your annual planning retreat happen is in the scheduling. Some people might have so much flexibility that it's easy to carve out an event of this scale on a whim, but most people probably do not. I recommend deciding on your annual planning retreat (dates, location, times, participants) as early as you can—perhaps by midyear the previous year, if that is feasible. Better yet, you can decide on making this an annual event and cordon off a standing one- or two-day block every single year. As for when in the year this should be scheduled, there is no one right answer! Some people love to be entirely finished with their planning by the start of the year and wish to protect the holiday season; in that case, early December could work. Others really prefer to be entirely in the fresh-start frame of mind that comes with the calendar shifting and might select the first Friday after January 1. Your annual planning session doesn't need to be in January—perhaps you and your partner like to plan the upcoming academic year with a session together in June, at the end of the school year. This approach might sync better for those in academia, with kids in school, or who have work schedules that are busier in winter months.

Retreat Structure

Now that you are convinced of the value of time set apart for this annual planning, it's time to set the agenda. Not everyone will want to include every activity and exercise mentioned here, but the ideas listed can be a jumping -off point for your retreat planning. (Yes, I recommend *planning* your planning retreat. I promise, this isn't as over-the-top as it sounds.)

Part 1: Get Relaxed and Spend Time Visioning

Our lives are hectic and most of us are not going to be in the right frame of mind to think freely about our deepest desires at the end of a long workday or immediately after school drop-off. Instead, many people benefit from an on-ramp of sorts. Try to engage in an activity that is relaxing but also gives you space to think and allow the constant logistical buzzing in your mind (unless that's just me?) to slow down a little bit. This activity could be a walk, a leisurely breakfast with your partner, a yoga session, doodling in a journal while sipping a cappuccino, or a ten-minute meditation. The specifics don't matter, and you can feel free to mix things up—just choose something to get you in a more open and calm state before you start planning in earnest.

Once you are ready, gather your favorite writing tools—it's time to get started with some visioning! You will be thinking but also capturing those thoughts in writing, so make sure you have your preferred set of supplies. You can use a notebook and lots of colored pens, or go with your laptop/tablet/electronic method of choice, with the caveat that paper may be better if you tend to get distracted by notifications and digital temptations.

Now, what *is* visioning? For our purposes here, visioning is a looser and dreamier version of planning. You're not thinking through a series of steps or thinking much about constraints, like limited time or finances. Instead, you are letting yourself think about what is possible in an ideal scenario: a dream future version of your life.

The first visioning exercise I recommend in your annual planning session is to zoom out. Even though this is an annual planning session and you will be eventually thinking through your year in very concrete terms, it's best to start with these broad strokes that clarify your ultimate hopes and dreams. So, start by taking the long view—I like either five or ten years into the future. To be clear, in this exercise I am not suggesting that you create a concrete plan for this wider time frame; for most people, there's simply too much uncertainty for that to be helpful. Instead, you're taking a more abstract approach to help you gain clarity on your biggest dreams and truest priorities.

In your long-term visioning, begin with the basics (the year, your age, ages of others in your family) and let your mind wander from there. These visions are going to be fuzzier and more dreamlike than anything you will be thinking of on shorter horizons, but they can be powerful. In fact, given the lack of certainty inherent in thinking about a five-year time frame, you are likely to let yourself open up and dream with more authenticity than you might otherwise. You are letting your brain off-leash to think about what you truly want, and what might be possible.

Questions you might ask yourself about life five or ten years into the future include:

- What do you look and feel like?
- Who do you spend the most time with? What are your relationships like?

- What do you do for work? For fun?
- Where are you living?
- What are you most proud of?
- What are you most excited about?
- What does a typical day look like for you?

After brainstorming about your ideal future, zoom in to the annual time frame. Pretend it's one year from now (write out the actual date!) and envision yourself looking back over the past twelve months. You can ask yourself the same questions, and perhaps add a few more, since there is less uncertainty in a twelve-month time frame. Potential additions might include:

- Which routines served you the most?
- Which events felt the most memorable and worthwhile?
- What was your greatest challenge, and how did you face it?
- What was your greatest achievement this year?
- What did you let go of?

These exercises aren't necessarily designed to point you in a specific direction. They certainly do not comprise a completed goals list for you to refer to over the next year—that would be impractical. Instead, by exploring your dreams in this more free and unlimited way, you will be more open to pursuing things that might have otherwise seemed too big or undefined. You are reminded of what really matters to you and can build on this abstract scaffold in the next part of your planning.

Finally, in your last visioning exercise, take a look back, rather than forward. In order to make effective plans, it's important to know where you are right now and to delve a bit into how you got there.

Maybe it's been a banner year for you and you are standing at the precipice of a new exciting phase in your life. Or perhaps the year was a slowly smoldering (or quickly combusting) dumpster fire. You might have health challenges to reckon with, unanswered dreams from the year before, disappointments to process, or all of the above. Moving brazenly forward without considering your current status and trajectory would be a mistake, so this is the time to think back and reflect.

There may be negative aspects, but I want to encourage you to remain as neutral as possible when you are doing this part. You can certainly celebrate your wins, but try to approach the challenges/losses/pivots/disasters with an air of curiosity rather than judgment. You aren't necessarily trying to problem-solve; just notice where things went awry or not according to last year's plan, if you had one!

Some questions to consider as you explore your experiences over the past twelve months:

- What went well this past year? (Note: humans have a strong negativity bias, so if you don't force yourself to find some positive aspects, you may miss them altogether!)
- What were your favorite experiences of the year?
- Who did you spend the most time with? How did these relationships feel?
- How would you sum up the past year in one sentence? One word?
- What, if anything, do you most regret doing or not doing?

- Which habits and routines worked for you? Which did not, and why?
- Which goals do you feel did not serve you—is there anything you are ready to let go?

Taken together, these exercises can take a good chunk of time! If you'd like to keep things on a schedule, consider twenty to thirty minutes of freewriting for each. You don't have to answer every question, but try not to shy away from those that might feel less comfortable. If you have extra time and are doing this retreat with a partner, it may be valuable to stop here and share some answers if it feels right.

Once you are done with your visioning, it will be time to move from the abstract and reflective to the concrete and practical. It's time to get out your calendar—but you can keep the colorful pens!

Part 2: Back to Reality: Understand Your Calendar Landscape

Why review your calendar when it's pretty unlikely that events twelve months away are set in stone? It's true that you may not know at this particular juncture what you'll be doing on, say, November 14. But at the same time, thinking about the big things that are likely to happen will provide a necessary grounding for your goals in the next step.

Some years are different from others. Maybe this is a highly work-focused year for you, with a big new project kicking off in April and a major conference in August. Or perhaps you already know that you will be moving, changing jobs, or welcoming a new baby to the family. Events of this scale are going to greatly impact the shape of your year as well as your available time and energy. Ultimately, you want to create a goals list that takes all of these important factors into account.

That said, sometimes smaller things matter, too. You may want to pay careful attention to beginnings and endings in the academic calendars that impact you—perhaps your own or those of your kids. There might be an exciting vacation you are looking forward to taking in June or a milestone birthday to celebrate.

Capturing these calendar items is essential. Not only will it help make your goal setting more realistic, but it may actually generate goals that relate to the events themselves—things you might have overlooked if you hadn't been thinking so far ahead.

The easiest way to take stock of these kinds of events is to create a page with the entire year on it. You can use a preprinted yearly calendar, or you can simply use a page (or sheet/note/document from the electronic modality of your choice) with all twelve months listed. Then, you can go through month by month and list as many things as you can think of. If it comes to mind, it's probably worth considering.

Here is a list of event types to help get you started:

- Transitions! Changes in housing, jobs, or life phases
- Birthdays and anniversaries. Yours, family members', close friends', or even that of a job or hobby. I celebrated the twentieth anniversary of my blog this year and had a lot of fun!
- Important dates on the academic calendar. This is not the time to catalog every single school closure (that will happen during

your seasonal planning!), but the start and end dates are probably significant, and the longer vacations, too.

- Holidays that are important to you
- Project due dates
- Any known travel
- Big events that pertain to other family members, like a giant project due date for your partner or your child's big performance, sports tournament, or music competition
- Days or weeks of unusual life or work commitment—for me, this includes my weeks on call, which are set over a year in advance. These impact my energy and ability to do other things, so it's helpful for me to have an awareness of when they are even as I set out to do annual planning.

This document may or may not become a working document for you. I have used an initial twelve-month calendar brain-dump page in starting to fill out my actual master calendar, but I've also recycled these lists once I've completed my annual planning retreat. The point isn't to actually *do* the scheduling of your summer trip right now—it's to have a complete (or as- complete-as-it-can-be) understanding of what you have up ahead that is already set over the next twelve months so you can take it into account during the next step. That said, if you have the time to be granular, you could certainly use it as a starting point for more detailed calendaring later on.

Once you've gotten a handle on the upcoming calendar landscape, this is a nice moment to take a pause and review your someday possibilities list, if you have one. The idea is not to scramble

Example Calendar Landscape Review

January

Work trip to NYC
2 weekend gym meets

February

C's birthday
Big Project due date

March

Spring break!
Half marathon
Speaking trip

April

Tax deadlines
A's birthday

May

Big Project due date

June

Goal marathon
School ends June 12
Summer course launch

July

Kids at camp 2 weeks
Trip to visit parents

August

Milestone anniversary!
Fun couples trip
Many school events

September

Family events

October

Busy work month
Leaf-peeping trip?

November

BLP Live
Thanksgiving

December

J + G birthdays!
Holidays – ski trip

to get all of these possibilities onto your list, but being reminded of them can be helpful as you move toward our next step of goal generation.

Part 3: Choose Your Domains and Generate Your List

You've arrived—it's now time to start capturing some goals! The combination of uninhibited visioning followed by a realistic calendar overview should have you beautifully primed to come up with exciting ideas for your next twelve months.

You might actually be surprised at how ready you feel, truthfully! In coaching parlance, there is a concept known as "the generative moment," a phenomenon where the client searching for answers is finally able to come up with a slew of ideas and possible solutions all at once. This is the aim for this step! That said, it's often helpful to begin with a bit of structure before you let loose with a freewheeling list of desires and goals. This can be accomplished fairly simply by beginning with choosing your domains.

In this context, domains are areas of life. Common domains are "work," "relationships," "self," and "community." Or you can be much more specific, with categories like "health," "new baby," "home environment," or "friendship." Your domains can be constant every single time you sit down to plan, or you can vary them by year or by season. There is no perfect number of domains, but I recommend somewhere between three and eight. Above that, things can get a bit confusing and unwieldy! I usually choose four to five.

The purpose of domains is twofold: first, constraints can be helpful for focusing our thinking, and second, identifying a given domain can ensure you elevate it and pay attention to it. When you are limited to a certain number of areas, you are less likely to have a deer-in-the-headlights feeling of overwhelm when it comes to choosing your goals. Instead, the domains themselves will likely lead you along lines of thinking about what is important to you in each area. For example, "work" will naturally lead you to think about next steps in your career, projects that excite you, or maybe relationships within the workplace. Furthermore, selecting a more specific category such as "health" ensures you will give it the attention you feel it deserves. (We know this, because you picked it!) With a health category, you may get more granular about which health-related goals you want to accomplish or the health-promoting habits you want to set. By naming it as a priority, you will expand and elaborate on your list, and it will be given the right amount of weight in your goal setting.

Example Domains

- Home
- Relationships
- Work
- Creative Projects
- Health
- Finance
- Spirituality
- Kids
- Adventures
- Learning
- Community
- Rest & Recovery

Setting up your domains typically is quick—there is no wrong way to identify your domains, and they are not set in stone! You can change them as the year goes on, cross off a domain in June if you decide it no longer serves you, or use entirely different domains in your seasonal planning (more about this to come, of course). Once you've made your selections, create a document of some kind to capture the ideas that are about to come. This can be as simple as a piece of printer paper divided into four quadrants (one for each domain—you can color code, too, if desired!) or a page or board for each domain in an app on your preferred device.

Once you have that set up, get geared up and ready to focus: your generative moment has arrived! This should be the meatiest and longest step in your annual goal-setting process. Let your ideas wash over you and record them into the appropriate domain bucket. Avoid censoring yourself; you'll be looking over and editing your list later. Just let yourself write down all of the things that you feel belong on this list—items to think about achieving or completing or perhaps changing in the coming year.

This will probably take a moderate length of time; perhaps between twenty and forty minutes. It might be surprising that you can effectively map out a year's biggest priorities in under an hour, but with the priming of the previous exercises and the dedicated time and space to do so, it is definitely possible—and likely will prove to be one of the most valuable hours of your year.

Part 4: Editing, Reframing, and Some Bonus Add-Ons

Now your list is created, but it's still considered a draft at this point! One round of edits and analysis will take that list from a set of great ideas to a workable, realistic, and functional blueprint for your year.

Before we dive into editing and possibly reframing some of your original selections, it's important to think a bit about the different kinds of goals out there. Thinking about ways to conceptualize and categorize goals can be helpful in making sure your goals fit your needs. In this step, go through each item on your draft list and decide if it fits one (or more) of the following categories. You can then keep it as is, reframe it, or add specifics.

The first category to look out for is habit goals, which are goals intended to be repeated. For any habit goal, it helps to specify exactly *what* the desired habit is and *how often* it will be performed. "I want to floss" sounds general but is a habit goal in disguise—you probably have a specific cadence in mind, and flossing once a month is likely not going to feel like a success. For habit goals, you can even add more detail if you find that helpful, such as the location or intended time of performing the habit.

Second, scan your list for time-sensitive goals. There are probably a number of items on your list that feel big enough to be on your yearly list but are anchored to a specific season or event. Examples of this kind of goal would be "plan my partner's fortieth birthday party." It's absolutely fine to keep these kinds of goals on your yearly list, but there's probably a clear time you needed to get started with this planning (especially if the birthday is in February!). Mark up the time-sensitive goals with an anticipated start date.

Next, look for goals that contain many complicated steps. In every annual goals list, there are probably a few that stand out as big projects. It's absolutely fine to include some of these on your list—after all, 365 is a sizable number of days! But it can still be helpful to perhaps give them a second look and see if they can be broken down into more approachable pieces. "Publish book" or "flip house" would be examples of project goals that could use some dissection. Go ahead and define the first big step in any multistage project and note that on your list. That way, when you are using this list to help generate your lower-tier (i.e., seasonal) lists later on, you already have an idea of a step that you can undertake in a reasonable time frame.

A fourth kind of goal to scan your list for is the foundation goal. This term was coined by author Gretchen Rubin and describes goals that are likely to help you in the achievement of all other goals. Some of them may also be habit goals; the common goal of getting more sleep fits into this category. It can be helpful to identify these and highlight them, because these kinds of goals will truly help you in building momentum with the rest of your intentions! Therefore, it makes sense to give them extra emphasis, especially at the start of the year.

Finally, any discussion of goal types would be incomplete without a mention of process goals versus outcome goals. Outcome goals are just what they sound like—goals based on the outcome of your work or intention. They are often out of your control. You can set a goal to qualify for the Boston Marathon, but the actual day might be blazing hot, leading you to miss your cutoff. Or maybe the race will be canceled like it was in 2020! Process goals, on the other hand, are centered around the anticipated actions to be taken, even if there is a desired outcome. Using our running example, the process version would be to train for your race with a weekly mileage goal or specific training plan in mind. Most people tend to focus on outcome goals when sometimes (not always, but sometimes!) a process goal would serve them better. Scan your list to see if there is any outcome goal that might be tweaked to place more emphasis on the journey or process.

Examples of Outcome Goals and Potential Corresponding Process Goals

OUTCOME GOAL	PROCESS GOAL
Run a 3:30 marathon.	Follow the Hanson Marathon Method, missing no more than 10 percent of prescribed workouts.
Lose ten pounds.	Eliminate soda and sweetened drinks; aim for adequate protein and a fruit or vegetable in each meal or snack.
Land an agent and book publishing contract.	Craft book proposal, obtain feedback from three colleagues, and send to agents.
Achieve a clutter-free home.	Create a list of the ten highest priority areas in your home to declutter. Using this list as a road map, go in order and clear out excess on a weekly basis for two hours each weekend.

Now you've analyzed your list and can spend a few more minutes editing and making final cuts. If there's something you are excited about that really doesn't seem to fit within the confines of the next year, you can move it to your someday possibilities list—the non-time-anchored parking lot of ideas we discussed in the previous chapter.

Before you move on to part 5, there's just one more audit process for your list: the fun audit! It's incredibly important that you have plenty of items on your list that make you smile—goals that spark joy! Our lives can be tough, but they are also finite. You want to ensure that you are enjoying yours—that is one of the core reasons for all of this in the first place! There is no scientific fun ratio out there (yet), but if you can, aim for a 2:1 fun/less fun ratio. You can set a goal to replace your hurricane windows, but only if you also plan to reconnect with your childhood BFF and take that photography class.

Part 5: Keep and Use Your List!

This part may seem obvious but cannot be overemphasized. You've just spent the better part of a day dreaming, scheming, drafting, and editing. And in truth, there is some value in just drawing up this list and going through the reflection necessary to create it. But to truly get the maximum benefit from all of this hard work, you need to put your list somewhere easily accessible, and you also need a plan for when you will look at it.

There is no perfect place for your list, but there are plenty of unwise ones. The latter category would include:

- Random pages in a nondescript notebook
- Your paper planner from the year prior
- A document saved haphazardly in "Documents"

You get the idea. Your list needs to be somewhere prominent and easily retrievable. I like to keep mine in both physical *and* digital forms. The physical form goes at the front of my planner for that year, and then I take pictures to save it digitally!

Other options are to have a dedicated goals planner, though that can be a commitment. You could also go digital only. This could then live at the top of your digital notes/filing system or even as your laptop background (for those bold goal setters who don't mind others peering at their lists). There are many variations on this theme, but the keys are (a) redundancy and (b) prominence.

As mentioned previously, having easy access to your list still isn't enough! It's amazing how we can get busy and just forget these things exist. But if we are waiting for a magical calm period to come along so we can check our list, we might be waiting many months (or forever). Instead, you will be using the nested goals method, which means that you will be getting this list out a minimum of once per season. We will delve deeply into seasonal planning in the next chapter, but a key step as you close your annual planning is to set the date and time of your next seasonal planning session—actually put it in the calendar. As an example, if you're completing your annual planning in January, be sure to set a time for seasonal planning two to three months down the road. We'll talk about more about seasonal planning and the strategic selection of these dates in the next chapter, but having a specific future time already reserved for reviewing this list is key. That way, you are guaranteed to see this list again and you will be able to reap all of the benefits of this extended annual planning session!

Your Annual Goals List: To Share or Not to Share?

No one plans in a vacuum. There may be some things on your list that are entirely individual, but in all likelihood many of the items involve others. If you are a parent, you may have multiple goals that involve your children or your shared pets or your shared living space.

Therefore, it is generally worthwhile to take some time to share your list...or at least the parts that you are comfortable sharing. If you have a partner, doing this whole exercise together with a celebratory dinner at the end can be a wonderful (and very fun!) way of kicking off a new year (or academic year or fiscal year—whatever your chosen twelve-month cycle is). This may provide a starting point to discuss logistics, or you may identify conflicts—probably better now than when you've already committed to something or gotten started. Finally, there's the value of accountability. I know this doesn't work for everyone, but many people find reporting back to others very powerful. In some cases, a friend rather than a partner may work better for accountability—they may be less directly involved and invested.

You could even consider formalizing this process by creating an accountability group of some kind. The group could meet three times yearly with the sharing of intentions followed by a midyear check-in and an end-of-year report session that also includes sharing goals for the following year. This could be general or specific to one area where you have required more support in the past, like creative work.

Celebrate and Get Excited!

Once you've completed this process, take time to acknowledge this effort! You're likely feeling ready for the start of a new year and excited to embark on your goals. Your annual goals list will be instrumental in helping you move through the next twelve months with more intention and momentum toward accomplishing the things you truly care about. The following checklist will help guide you and ensure you don't miss a beat in your annual planning process.

Annual Planning Checklist: Your Own Planning Retreat!

Logistics

- ☐ Decide on the format, location, length, and participants of your annual planning retreat.
- ☐ Schedule it directly into your calendar. Book any associated accommodations if you will be doing this away from your home or workplace.

Inner Work: Visioning + Reflection

- ☐ **Five-to-ten-year visioning exercise.** Envision yourself five or ten years in the future. Ask yourself specific questions about what life would look like if things were going very well for you.
- ☐ **One year ahead visioning exercise.** Reflect on this date one year into the future. From that vantage point, explore what you are most proud of and happy about. Get specific on the steps you took to achieve these wins.
- ☐ **Looking back reflection exercise.** Spend some time reflecting on the previous twelve months, including a celebration of what went well and an exploration of what didn't serve you.

Back to Reality: Overview of Your Calendar Landscape

- ☐ **Identify important events and commitments up ahead.** Note important dates that are already known, from holidays and birthdays to big work deadlines. Create a one-page summary of the year showing these mountain ranges already set in your calendar landscape.

- ☐ **Review your someday possibilities list, if you have one.** This is a great time to have these ideas fresh in your mind in case any of them feel right for the coming year.

List Generation: Your Generative Moment

- ☐ **Choose your domains.** Decide which categories you will use for your annual goals. These can be fairly general (as in "personal" and "work") or more specific ("health" or "spirituality"). Aim for between three and eight domains.
- ☐ **Generate your goals!** Without censoring, let yourself list the goals that come to your mind for the year time frame.
- ☐ **Audit and refine.** Scan your list, noting where you have certain kinds of goals (habit goals, time-sensitive goals, foundation goals, process goals, and outcome goals). Edit or reframe as needed. If there are items on the list that excite you but just don't seem to be in the cards for the upcoming year, move them to your someday possibilities list.

Post-Retreat: Getting the Most out of Your Goal-Setting Efforts

- ☐ **Save your list somewhere prominent and easily accessible.** Consider a digital copy even if you love to plan on paper.
- ☐ **Consider sharing your goals.** Share with a partner to discuss logistics and feasibility or with a friend for accountability and support. Some might even enjoy sharing and following up in a group setting.
- ☐ **Decide on the next time you will look at this list!** If you are following the nested goals method, you will be reviewing your annual

list at every seasonal planning session. If you are just getting started with annual planning, create an appointment with yourself one to two months into the future to review this list. If you have lost lists like this in the past, include details about where the list lives on that appointment note. Feel free to create extra copies—redundancy is welcome here!

Quintiles, Trimesters, and Planning Within Your Seasons

In the last chapter, annual planning was covered in detail, and hopefully you are now armed with a very thoughtful list of goals and dreams for the year. Taking a step back, let's imagine for one moment what it would be like if annual planning was your one and only dedicated goal-setting and planning session each year. Many people do, in fact, take plenty of time at the start of the year to reflect and resolve, and then they stop there. To be honest, I was one of those people for many years! Often, in January, I wrote out detailed lists in a notebook (or posted passionate manifestos on my old-school blog), but the follow-up was sorely lacking. Creating one thoughtful plan and hoping it will buoy you for a 365-day stretch is wishful thinking at best. The key to creating lasting momentum throughout your year (and really, your life!) is to have effective systems for each time horizon, linking big-picture visions to daily tasks. This way, plans can flex according to life's unpredictable path and align with real-life challenges as they unfold.

So where exactly do you go from your annual planning extravaganza to create this continuity? The next logical time horizon level below annual planning is the *season*, and this is where I love to use the quintile! This is just one option, though. You might prefer the quarter; many traditional systems divide the year into quarters, and some physical planners are even designed with the quarter in mind. The concept of dividing up the year into smaller chunks is a great one, but these dividing points are arbitrary.

So what exactly is a quintile? It may not (yet!) be a commonly used term, but I hope it will resonate with some of you as much as it has with me. One day, I was trying to figure out why dividing the year into traditional quarters felt off to me. With multiple school-age kids, I noticed that my year absolutely contained its own naturally embedded cut points—they just didn't fall in regular three-month intervals. Instead, my life rhythms seemed to ebb and flow with the school calendar. I was trying to disregard this and divide the year into four parts when I suddenly realized that I didn't have to! Pregnancies are famously divided into trimesters, as are some university systems. My year could be divided into three, four, or really any number of segments that made sense.

I took out my calendar and thought about where the dividing lines felt most natural for me in that particular phase of life. January 1 always feels like a fresh start to me, so I wanted Q1 to begin there. The school year goes until early June where we live, but that stretch seemed quite long, so I decided to split it into two with spring break—a nice dividing line, especially since April and May tend to have a busier energy in many places. The end of school clearly ushered in a new set of routines and challenges, so I defined Q3 as the weeks my kids were off from school, coinciding with most of summer. Once again, lifestyles and schedules shifted drastically in my household around mid-August with back-to-school defining the start of Q4. But like January to June, August to December loomed long, and I noted that there is definitely a special celebratory spark in the air that begins in November. November 1 became the start of my Q5, and the concept of quintiles was born!

The quintiles concept resonates with many. I've even heard some people refer to my systems as a "quintiles system" of planning—but this is a bit of a misnomer. For me, dividing the year this way makes so much sense, and it feels right to engage in a relatively detailed planning season to kick off each of these five seasons. For others, though, this may be entirely off the mark! So, while I am excited to share this one particular method for dividing up the year, I want to emphasize that the key is not in the quintiles themselves, but rather figuring out the right seasons for you right now.

For planning purposes, your defined seasons can be anything you want them to be! They don't have to be equal in length, and the number you choose is up to you—but I suggest something in the ballpark of three to six. A college student may feel that four seasons works well, but not the four equal quarters that some corporate systems use. Perhaps season one is the fall semester, season two is winter break (long at some universities!), season three is spring semester, and season four is time off over the summer. Alternatively, a physician in residency training might divide up their year based on the rotations or training blocks coming up ahead, and an author might choose to divide the year into seasons based on their main work activity, whether it is drafting a proposal, writing, editing, or promoting a new work. There are countless variations, but you probably get the point by now: choose seasons that make sense for the flow of your life at this particular phase.

3 Ways to Define Your Seasons

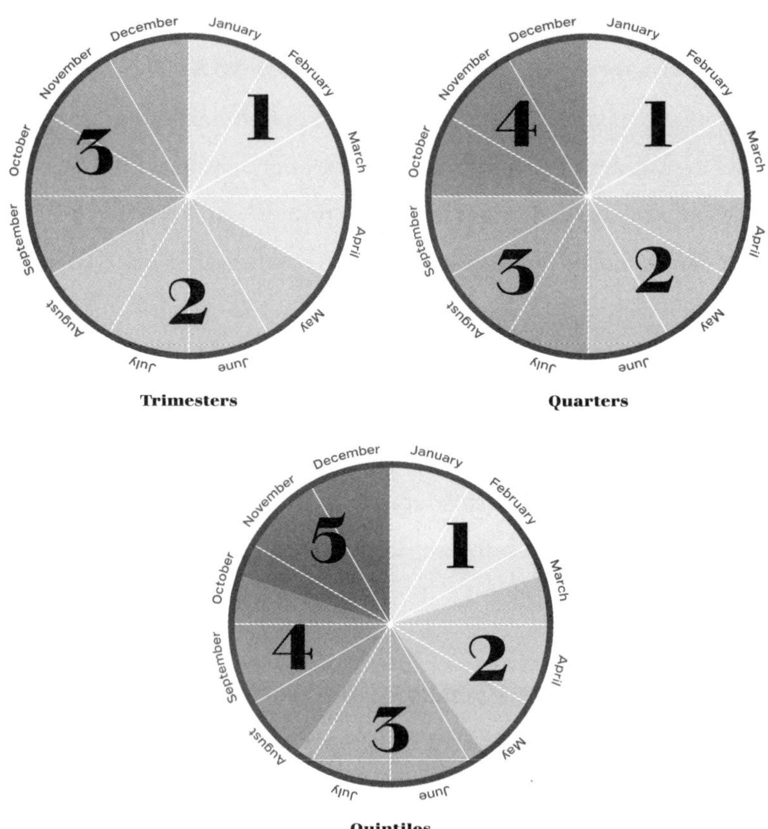

Seasonal Planning: A Mini-Retreat

Once you've defined your seasons, you've given yourself the gift of anywhere between three and six fresh starts over the course of the year. You've also uncovered the most useful and natural points in the year to spend time reflecting and planning the months ahead. You invested a lot of time and careful thought into creating your annual goals list, after all! Seasonal planning (and later, carrying these plans forward at smaller and smaller time horizons) will bring your dreams and ideas one step closer to fruition.

This time, though, you may not have an entire weekend to devote to reflection and planning. Understandable, since taking two days away from your regular responsibilities to plan five times over the course of the year would certainly start to add up, and most people probably want to enjoy vacations that aren't centered around planning (though I wouldn't judge if you love those, too!). This works out, though! Since you're thinking through a smaller time frame and you've already built a scaffold during your annual planning session, seasonal planning can be done in a lower-key fashion.

For most people, it is realistic to complete a solid and fairly comprehensive seasonal planning session in a half day. You can be creative with this, too! If you don't have the freedom to just put "STRATEGIC PLANNING" on your work calendar and disappear for an afternoon, this time can be broken up into smaller chunks (perhaps an hour midday for a few days in a row?) or found on a weekend, in one or two sessions at a local coffee shop.

Seasonal planning includes a detailed goal-setting session, and the next several sections will delve into how to effectively set and capture your priorities for the next season. Then, other helpful seasonal practices will be discussed, from building your ideal week to zeroing in on routines and making sure to include things that you find truly fun.

Seasonal Planning Part 1: Reflection

Just like with your annual session, you will begin with some reflection—it's hard to choose a future direction without reflecting a bit on your current status! You can think through these prompts, but I highly recommend getting your thoughts down in writing. Your notes may or may not be something you will look back on, but the act of choosing what to write down will help organize your thinking, so grab either a notebook and pen or your device of choice and try not to censor yourself too much! You might not have as much time to relax your mind as you would during a dedicated annual planning retreat, but even a few minutes sitting quietly and thinking about the purpose of your session can be helpful to get you in the right mindset for reflection without judgment.

Begin with looking back at your last season. If this is the very first time you are conducting a seasonal planning session, you may not have a previous seasonal list to look at, but next time you will! For your very first session, you can just holistically reflect back on the past few months. Start on a positive note with your successes, as many of us tend to forget to celebrate the things that went well. You can then go through any goals you set or ideas you had for the season and decide whether any undone things are worth moving forward into the current season or not. If not, you have two options: you can table them (for a future season this year, or into the indefinite future), or you can let them go.

For items that you feel are important enough to move into your upcoming season, spend a little more time thinking about what happened last season. Were there barriers present in the previous quarter that will be gone in the next? If so, great! But if not, you will have to dig a bit deeper to determine what might need to change to help you be successful in the coming season.

To illustrate the importance of this kind of analysis, I will share my own mildly embarrassing struggle to complete our family's basic wills and estate planning. Since I understood the importance of getting it done, estate planning made its way into my annual lists year after year. This goal would get as far as the seasonal level, but since it's not a terribly fun topic to think about, I neglected to troubleshoot the barriers I was facing that were preventing it from getting checked off—and thus I kept seeing it over and over again, without any progress made. I finally recognized that what was missing was a firm deadline and professional assistance, and I was able to (finally) check off this important goal once I changed my goal from the vague and scary "do estate planning" to "set up meeting to review documents with husband and an estate-planning lawyer." I needed a dedicated time slot and the expertise and time pressure of an outsider, and until these elements were added, I was unlikely to move forward on this goal, even though it was something I clearly wanted to finish.

Options for Incomplete Seasonal Goals

Seasonal Planning Part 2: Annual Goals Review

Once you've reviewed the last season's goals, it's time to bring out your annual list. YES, this means that you'll be seeing that list every season or a minimum of three to six times per year! This in itself can be a game changer for many who get all fired up around the new year but never revisit their detailed plans again.

Side note: I have noticed that some people get a little bit squeamish about goals lists or maybe even the concept of goals in general. One friend of mine who identifies as a bit of a perfectionist tends to avoid goals (and definitely goals lists!) like the plague because she hates the way it makes her feel when she doesn't complete all of them. This seems like an opportune moment to note that these lists are just lists. They are ideas, not mandates. They are a set of thoughts you've captured, not a life report card. They are there to help you prioritize, not to determine your priorities for you. When you pull out your annual list, I do not want you to cast judgment on your previous self (for setting such crazy goals!) or your current self (for not getting them finished).

Try your best to instead see your goals list for what it is: a set of possibilities that you made one day when you were thinking about what you wanted in life, at that particular moment. It's okay for your priorities to shift, and thus it is completely natural and expected for you to *not* do some of the things you thought about and wrote down. When you cast this light on your list, I hope you can view it with an openness and interest and not dread the practice in any way.

Viewing your annual goals list, you may find yourself having an impulse to cram as many of the items into your upcoming season as possible. This can be normal, but try to resist and proceed calmly and with intention. Your scan is to see if anything resonates with you right now and feels like it fits well with the upcoming season. Sometimes, items will stand out just due to time constraints; for example, if your father's seventieth birthday is in August and your goal is to throw a big party for him, this goal is probably going to wind up on your summer list if you haven't tackled it by then! Goals may also land on your seasonal list because they just seem right for the time, or you find yourself excited about them. Personally, I might be more interested in household organization projects in quintile one and quintile four (new year/back-to-school seasons) than I am in the spring. Scan your list, write down the items that seem like they might belong in the upcoming season, and don't think too much about the rest!

Depending on how much bandwidth you feel you have in a given season, this can be an opportune time to revisit your someday possibilities list. You can skip it if you are already starting to feel overwhelmed, but if the season feels expansive and you are looking for ideas, that is a great place to start!

Seasonal Planning Part 3: Look Ahead, Around, and Within

You may be itching to make new goals at this point! You're starting to think about the upcoming season, and you already have ideas from the last season. You're going to CRUSH those undone goals, because clearly the months to come are completely devoid of other commitments and activities, right? After all, it's the FUTURE!

Except this definitely isn't the way futures tend to unfold when they become the present. And what Future You has on his or her plate is worth considering, because it is going to impact your ability to move forward with various things. This isn't a bad thing, by the way. It just *is* and should be considered in a calm and nonjudgmental way before you decide on your desired commitments for the coming months. You may be about to give birth to twins (double congratulations!) in the next couple of weeks, and with that in mind you'll probably have a very different level of free time and bandwidth compared to an empty nester starting a sabbatical. Myriad levels of commitment and energy lie between these two extremes, and it's important to take stock of where you are and what you have coming up.

Pull out your master calendar, and take a few minutes to review the coming season's commitments that are already scheduled. Then, go a step beyond and think about items that may not be captured (even if your master calendar is generally up-to-date, you may not have thought of every single birthday, family celebration, or work project due date). Write them down in a format that allows you to see the big picture—I like a one-page printout with multiple months listed on it, either just as sections of the page or in a calendar format. Feel free to color code any big things you see—trips away from home, big celebrations, major due dates—anything that helps you understand your level of commitment and busyness over the coming weeks.

Then, take this one fuzzier step forward and reflect on how you feel and how you generally tend to feel in a given season. Are you recovering from an illness or previous stressful event and feeling the need to lie low? Do you have an infant that is not sleeping, and it's making you incredibly tired? Are you bursting with excitement about an upcoming project or holiday? Do you absolutely hate your area's summer weather with a fiery passion? (Okay, I might be projecting with this one.) You may have several thoughts and some of them may be conflicting, but it's still helpful to jot them down. It does not make sense to plan a season filled with go getter, pie-in-the-sky reach goals if you are ready to hunker down and hibernate, and, on the flip side, if you find yourself raring to go, it's best to know that so you can ramp up quickly!

Looking Ahead for the Season

January

Back to school after 2 weeks off

Initial draft due January 15th

Regular gymnastics meets start up

February

C's birthday!

Call week

Speaking trip February 26th

Final due date for manuscript

March

Half marathon

Podcast recording retreat

Soccer tournament

Kids – spring break!

Feelings / Focus for the Season

Biggest professional focus: **Writing and completing manuscript**

Biggest home focus: Functional back-to-school routines + supporting kids In their sports during this full season

Seasonal Planning Part 4: Choose Your Domains and Generate Your List

Does this sound familiar? It might, because this step is exactly the same as the one taken at the annual level. The difference is that scope of your goals will become narrower, since you are choosing things you hope to accomplish within a shorter time frame.

Just like with your annual planning, it helps to identify your domains first. You can use the same domains every single season, if you'd like! Some people prefer to do this, perhaps choosing domains that reflect their highest values. Others enjoy shifting things around to match the feel of the upcoming season, choosing a domain like "celebrate" for a holiday-heavy period. Whatever your choices, selecting domains of some kind is helpful, in part because it helps provide some organization to your brainstorming and also because you're less likely to neglect an area of life that is important to you.

Integrating elements to generate your seasonal goals list

Once you've chosen, your generative moment has (again) arrived! This is the meatiest part of your seasonal planning session, and you should let yourself capture whatever feels right within each domain without too much self-censorship—you can always edit later! You will be integrating from three main sources here: your prior seasonal review, your annual goals list, and your notes about what is up ahead, including the concrete (scheduled events/deadlines/calendar landscape) and the more abstract (your energy and a more holistic sense of how you are feeling).

Seasonal Planning Part 5: Save Your List and Start to Act

Once you have your seasonal list, decide where it will be kept. I like to have my seasonal list relatively close at hand, since I know I'll be referring to it monthly at the very least. Many people also find it useful to keep seasonal lists from years past, as things happen in cycles and a one-year-old list can be a nice reference for you in the future. As the goals on this list are usually getting a bit more specific (as compared to annual goals), it can be helpful to start thinking about them in more concrete terms, and consider adding items directly to your calendar to ensure you get things started within your intended time frame.

If one of your seasonal goals centers around an upcoming trip, for example, you might want to go ahead and put a task on your calendar to book your flights and hotel. You don't have to get super granular and address every single item you included, because you'll be doing that on smaller time-horizon scales! But if you have time, you can give yourself a little jump start where it makes sense to do so, building some momentum into the beginning of your season.

Congratulations—if you've followed the recommendations in the chapter thus far, you have completed a comprehensive seasonal goal-setting procedure! This practice is at the core of seasonal planning, but there are other aspects of planning and thinking through your upcoming season that can be incredibly helpful in allowing you to live with less reactivity and more ease.

Your Ideal Week

I know! We are dealing with seasons in this chapter. Why would the time frame of *just one week* come into play already? Bear with me. There will be lots of discussion of planning at the weekly level coming up, I promise (see chapter 5), but I believe that the Ideal Week exercise comprises an integral part of your seasonal planning routine.

I first learned about the Ideal Week concept from Michael Hyatt, a former CEO turned productivity coach and author of *Free to Focus*,[1] among other books about time management. Michael developed the Full Focus Planner as a physical planning tool to help bring his techniques to life for his clients, and one of its signature spreads is titled "Ideal Week." The idea is simple yet powerful: draw out an ideal week for your upcoming quarter, showing how you would like to be spending your hours from 5:00 a.m. Monday for the next 168 hours.

The Ideal Week is not a blueprint for your actual schedule, as most weeks are not ideal. Case in point: the typing of this section has been interrupted three times because I have a child home sick, and this event was nowhere to be found in my Ideal Week fantasies! However, it's still incredibly useful to put pen to paper (or stylus to tablet) and map out all of the moving parts in your upcoming season. This will achieve several aims.

First, you will be able to see if and when your seasonal goals will actually fit into your calendar (and by extension, your life). This might lead to a reality check or an adjustment somewhere. If you are hoping to make this a season of strength training but find there are no swathes of free time large enough for gym visits, you have a few options: you could adjust your work hours or change your childcare situation to open up more time, plan on more streamlined home workouts, or table this fitness endeavor to a future season. None of these strategies is "right," but all are better than entering a season with exciting goals but no practical ability to carry them out. Mapping things out in the concrete format of an Ideal Week forces you to face these facts and anticipate challenges.

Second, you will likely come up with logistical ideas. We spend so much time living our lives and rarely take a pause to take a formal look at how all of the pieces come together. Seeing things laid out this way three to six times yearly is your chance to ask questions about your routines, big and small. Do those weekly meetings *have* to take an hour each, or could they be reimagined as briefer check-ins? Is there a way you could make your commute more enjoyable with an audiobook or podcast series? If you note that you spend five hours per week blow drying your hair, is there a way to change your hairstyle or hair expectations to streamline this? (Personally, I get Japanese-straightening done twice a year solely to avoid the time suck of hairstyling!)

Next, you will get a chance to ensure you have created an Ideal Week you are (at least somewhat) looking forward to! When you look over this idealized week and think about the upcoming season, you will

Template for sketching out your Ideal Week

Monday	Tuesday	Wednesday
12a	12a	12a
1a	1a	1a
2a	2a	2a
3a	3a	3a
4a	4a	4a
5a	5a	5a
6a	6a	6a
7a	7a	7a
8a	8a	8a
9a	9a	9a
10a	10a	10a
11a	11a	11a
12p	12p	12p
1p	1p	1p
2p	2p	2p
3p	3p	3p
4p	4p	4p
5p	5p	5p
6p	6p	6p
7p	7p	7p
8p	8p	8p
9p	9p	9p
10p	10p	10p
11p	11p	11p
12a	12a	12a

Thursday	Friday	Saturday	Sunday
12a	12a	12a	12a
1a	1a	1a	1a
2a	2a	2a	2a
3a	3a	3a	3a
4a	4a	4a	4a
5a	5a	5a	5a
6a	6a	6a	6a
7a	7a	7a	7a
8a	8a	8a	8a
9a	9a	9a	9a
10a	10a	10a	10a
11a	11a	11a	11a
12p	12p	12p	12p
1p	1p	1p	1p
2p	2p	2p	2p
3p	3p	3p	3p
4p	4p	4p	4p
5p	5p	5p	5p
6p	6p	6p	6p
7p	7p	7p	7p
8p	8p	8p	8p
9p	9p	9p	9p
10p	10p	10p	10p
11p	11p	11p	11p
12a	12a	12a	12a

hopefully feel an overall positive sense of anticipation. Some nerves are normal if there are big changes up ahead, but the best possible version of your schedule should not fill you with trepidation or dread. Yes, this is yet another fun audit. If you don't see anything built into your week that looks truly enjoyable for you, I recommend going back to the drawing board to figure out where you can add a slice of peace or social time or whatever you feel would serve you best in the coming season. It's definitely true that some life stages allow for more of this than others, but in most cases, you can at least build in some tiny bright spots, whether it's a social lunch once a week or a night where you look forward to takeout along with a favorite show.

This exercise can be conducted at any time, but seasonally is a natural cadence, because our routines often change as we segue into a new season. For parents of school-aged children this is particularly true, but even without school schedules each season is likely to have its own emphasis and feel, with weather and patterns of light impacting our rhythms: your average midsummer week is probably going to differ significantly from your December weeks. Finally, three to six times per year seems about right to check in on your overall schedule and think about how the pieces are fitting together. We spend much of our time existing within these frameworks, so it makes sense to take some time to ensure it is built to serve you and not the other way around.

The template on the previous pages is the one I personally fill out each season, and the one I encourage course participants to try as well.

Reminder: Make sure to include time for planning and task management in your own Ideal Week, since these activities do take time!

Finances: Seasonal Assessment

This is not a book about finances, and you definitely do not want me advising you on the optimal ratio of stocks to bonds in your retirement portfolio. However, a planning system that does not include some kind of practical and realistic financial assessment would be incomplete. In general, to accomplish many things, there are two essential ingredients: time and money. Of the two, I consider time to be more precious, as it is irreplaceable, and because many of the most important things in life really are free (or priceless, depending on how you look at them!). That said, having enough money around is still quite useful when it comes to efficiency and proactivity, and some life dreams simply require cash! So, thinking about your spending (and saving) habits at the seasonal level is worthy of discussion. Why seasonally? A year is a bit too long to course-correct if things are going in the wrong direction, and expenses vary enough month to month that a season seems like a more reasonable time frame to conduct a broad overview.

I am not naturally a saver, nor am I particularly gifted at managing money. I am generous to myself and others, and when I was younger the only thing I considered doing with the earnings from my babysitting jobs (and later, working for a video store and a test-prep company) was spending them. I went to Europe after my senior year with a credit card and zero concept of how I would pay the bill when it came—thankfully, the hostels I stayed in were pretty inexpensive and my parents bailed me out (but they noted this was absolutely a one-time deal—and it was!).

A decade and change later (years that included many nights of little sleep and beeping pagers, plus our first baby!), my husband and I finished with medical training and began working at our first "real" jobs as physicians. Suddenly, we had paychecks that looked pretty substantial, especially when compared to the ones we received in residency. I thought to myself, *Great! This is more money than I can even imagine spending, and I'm sure it will just accumulate without having to think about it. What will we even* do *with it?*

The answer: plenty. We had two more children, bought a home in an expensive zip code, hired a nanny, and said "yes" to plenty of pricey things we couldn't do as residents. We did pay off some loans and thankfully were wise enough to avoid debt, other than our low-interest mortgage, but we saved very little. One night, six or so years into our "real jobs" lifestyle, my husband and I sat down to calculate our net worth for the first time and it was disappointing, if not a little bit shocking. We had been working hard, both of us at full-time jobs complete with call responsibilities, and THIS was the outcome!? Neither of us planned to stop working particularly early, but at that moment our projected retirement date could be estimated at approximately "never."

Something clearly had to change, and our seasonal finance meetings were born. We also started tracking our day-to-day finances more closely (more on that in the next chapter), but every three months we began sitting down to look at all of our account balances, from retirement accounts to college savings to our mortgage. (Note: we chose actual quarters for this in lieu of the quintiles I use for the rest of my seasonal planning, just because this seemed to more appropriately reflect the fiscal calendar.) These four yearly automatic checkpoints have become a natural forum for discussion of what is going well or what might need to change about our spending habits and lifestyle.

There are many ways to conduct a financial or net-worth audit, but ours is just a simple spreadsheet with a listing of accounts. Every quarter, we put in the updated balances and add up the total. Some debate whether home value should be included, but we do, subtracting the amount owed on our mortgage from the current valuation on real-estate sites. For fun (and motivation), we plug the number into a "Years to Financial Independence" calculator created by famed financial blogger Mr. Money Mustache.[2]

Once we started doing this, our net worth began increasing incrementally and is now much more in line with what I might have hoped for at this point in our careers. I wish we had started doing this many years before we did, as I believe it might have made a significant impact on our most important financial choices (prime example: we no longer live in such a pricey zip code!). Looking over your own balance sheet isn't an automatic ticket to building wealth, but cultivating awareness in this realm is still helpful.

On the flip side, one of the reasons I enjoy doing this big-picture look seasonally is that it means we can generally *not* think about it the rest of the time. Meetings like this can be stressful, especially during times when maybe the account balances aren't quite where you were hoping they would be. But by giving it a dedicated spot for regular check-ins, you'll be able to address things enough without spending excess time ruminating about it (or even avoiding it and then having guilt around avoiding it—trust me, I've been there!).

If you don't have a partner to meet with, this meeting could be done solo or with a financial professional. (This is outside the scope of this book, but just be very careful and do a thorough vetting if you choose to go that route!)

Seasonal Planning Wild Cards: Choose Your Own Adventure!

Setting seasonal goals, filling out an Ideal Week template, and some kind of financial reckoning are applicable to almost anyone looking to implement a comprehensive planning system. However, you may have needs that extend beyond these elements, and this is where the customization component comes in! In my Best Laid Plans Academy course, one of the main goals is to help participants craft their own agendas for planning rituals at every time horizon.[3] I provide plenty of ideas (and often some pretty strong recommendations!) but acknowledge that each person is going to have their own unique planning needs, and these needs may vary across one's lifespan.

A brand-new parent may not be excited about planning elaborate travel over the next few months, and a retiree probably doesn't need to do a deep dive into their personal time off (PTO) usage. That said, it's helpful to decide what does apply so that you can include it with regularity each season. This next section contains some common components to seasonal planning—you can choose which ones make sense for you or use them as inspiration to come up with your own!

Childcare Audit

If you have children, this is an important component to address seasonally. Some seasons, things will be simple—maybe everyone is still in day care and things are going well, no changes needed! But many times, there will be transitions that need to be navigated and gaps that need to be figured out. It's best to look at your upcoming season *and* do a brief survey of the season ahead, or maybe even two seasons ahead if we're talking about the camp signups that seem to get earlier and earlier every year! Include both regular care and backup options in your audit, and think about whether you have reliable babysitters (hired or family) you could call if needed.

Travel Planning

This can be a fun category to consider seasonally, both at the big-picture level and from a practical standpoint (booking flights, hotels, etc.). My friend Kelsey Wharton came up with something she calls the "Years Are Short" family spreadsheet, which details her family's travel dreams years in advance.[4] She includes her kids' ages, various family milestones, and the trips she hopes they will take together. This might help motivate you to save for a trip that feels important and could be looked at and updated seasonally.

On a more practical level, travel is similar to childcare in that in many ways it helps to look at the upcoming season plus the one after that, assessing whether anything needs to be planned, booked, or budgeted for. You can even use this time to create reminders for yourself about making reservations that need to happen closer to travel dates (restaurants, activities, etc.). This is included in my own seasonal planning session, and I have to admit it's one of my favorite parts, as the anticipation just adds to the fun and it's so much easier to book a hotel six months out than it is to try to snag one at the last minute.

Seasonal Household Maintenance

Similar to finances, I am no home maintenance expert, and as a Floridian I have exactly zero winterizing knowledge to impart—however, I know to check on hurricane supplies every June! Many household maintenance activities occur predictably each season. You can do a quick search to provide ideas that might apply to your home and region, and if you do create lists of seasonal tasks, these are lists to save somewhere permanent, as they will inevitably come around each year. If you live alone or are the main "manager" of these sorts of tasks for your household, this category may be an important one to include in your seasonal planning.

Meeting Worthiness

Most of the meetings that end up on our calendars on a regular basis aren't new. They're there because someone once put them there and checked the "weekly" box on the scheduling app, and now they exist in that format in perpetuity, unless someone actively decides to change it.

The seasonal level is a reasonable time frame to determine the worthiness of each of your recurring meetings or obligations. This needn't be limited to work—you can also look at your weekly run club meetup and the PTO sessions you attend. Some of this may be addressed during your Ideal Week exercise, but adding it in as a separate element could give it even more weight. You might decide that all of your meetings are perfect for the season, and that's great! But entering this with a start-from-scratch mindset, you might wonder if an hour is really necessary for Friday's team check-in. Would you make it an hour *now* if you were starting from scratch? Maybe, and maybe not. You want each meeting to prove its worthiness of a dedicated slot on your calendar!

Wardrobe Assessment

The weather changes seasonally, our lifestyles often shift seasonally, and our clothes…well, if you're anything like me, they tend to lag behind. Some people would benefit from adding a wardrobe assessment in seasonally because they love fashion and style, and others (those more like me) might love it for the exact opposite reason—perhaps they can address it just once, order some weather-appropriate staples, and not think about clothing for the next few months.

If there are children's clothes to contend with, this poses another challenge, as kids grow out of things and it can be amusing (or annoying) to realize that last year's winter clothes are significantly too small right as the first chill hits. By building a family wardrobe assessment into your seasonal routine, you can get ahead of this potential reactivity trap.

Media Query

Have you ever found out about a concert right before it happens in your area—when the tickets are all sold out and there's no hope of finding childcare in time? It's happened to me on more than one occasion, and yet one of my favorite things to do is to see my favorite artists live. One season, I did a quick search to see who was playing nearby and realized this simple habit could be a game changer—making it much easier for me to have these experiences, which often turn out to be some of my most memorable of the year.

Maybe concerts aren't your thing, but instead you're a movie buff or you love going to hot new restaurants, or binge-watching your favorite series right when it comes out. A media query (just search something like "new TV series coming out June, July, August" of the current year) can quickly show you what you have to look forward to. This can potentially add to the fun, whether it's just in the form of anticipation (anticipatory fun still counts as fun!) or the ability to plan something more elaborate like a watch party.

Meal Planning and Pantry Investigation

We all have to eat, but everyone has their own approach to meal planning (or serendipitous meal concoction, as the case may be). That said, most of us end up with some sort of weekly rhythm around shopping and many of us have foods that become seasonal staples: stews in winter, pumpkin everything in the fall, or grilled delicacies in the summer. If meal planning is stressful for you, you may want to consider doing some of it seasonally. Kendra Adachi of Lazy Genius fame has described something she calls a "meal matrix," which is essentially a template of weekly meals.[5] This is something that can be decided once (one of her tenets is exactly that: "Decide Once") and then held for a season. If this approach is inspiring to you, adding a meal planning element to your seasonal planning might be helpful. Alternatively, seasonally would be a great cadence for assessing the contents of your freezer and pantry to determine what needs to be used up.

Seasonal Reading Lists

If you are a reader, you probably have a TBR ("to be read") list. It can enhance your reading life to have a TBR list filled with titles that you are excited to read and that feel right for the time of year. Seasonal rhythms work well for creating or refreshing your TBR list—you might update it regularly or curate lists for specific times of the year. Summer reading lists filled with juicy novels are a classic choice, or perhaps you gravitate toward personal-development nonfiction in the first quarter of the year.

This concludes our discussion of seasonal planning. Whether you plan to conduct it in quarters, trimesters, or quintiles, you will welcome these intermittent fresh starts embedded into your year. Now, we will move our focus down one time horizon—on to the month!

Seasonal Planning Checklist

Preparation

- ☐ **Define your seasons:** quarters, trimesters, quintiles, or whatever you'd like! Aim to segment the year into three to six pieces that fit the rhythms of your life.
- ☐ **Logistics:** Ensure you have about a half day blocked up for your seasonal planning. Alternatively, you can divide this into two or more sessions if that's more practical! You can also consider doing this with a friend or partner.

Goal Setting

- ☐ **Reflection:** Look back at the previous season, celebrate your wins, troubleshoot struggles, and decide what, if anything, to migrate forward.
- ☐ Review your annual goals list and consider checking in with your someday possibilities list if you're feeling ready for more ideas.
- ☐ Look ahead, around, and within: evaluate your calendar, current goings-on, and assess your own energy levels and overall mood.
- ☐ Choose your domains and generate your list.
- ☐ Save your list and consider setting the groundwork for some of your biggest priorities.
- ☐ Think about the next action for bigger projects.
- ☐ Put key tasks directly into your master calendar.

Seasonal Planning Beyond Goals

- ☐ Complete the Ideal Week exercise.
- ☐ Conduct a seasonal financial assessment.
- ☐ Additional “wild card” aspects of seasonal planning: choose any that apply!
    - Childcare audit
    - Travel planning
    - Seasonal household maintenance
    - Meeting worthiness audit
    - Wardrobe assessment
    - Media query
    - Meal planning and pantry investigation
    - Seasonal reading lists

The Month, or Your Twelve Yearly Clean Slates

Twelve times every year, your motivation gets a boost in the form of a monthly fresh start. This has actually been studied and officially named "The Fresh Start Effect" by Wharton economists.[1] They found that aspirational online searches (for "gym visit," as an example) spiked at certain time points, including the beginning of each week, month, year, or even the participant's birthday. They postulated that these landmark dates serve as natural points of reckoning and can help increase motivation, especially for aspirational behaviors.

It's fairly common knowledge that this happens at the start of each year, but one brief motivated and productive streak every 365 days has a limited overall impact. By emphasizing the fresh-start powers of each month, however, one might imagine how this could approach significance. Even if efforts peter out by month's end, ten days of strong motivation amounts to 120 days out of 365—not too shabby!

I know that I personally benefit from paying a lot of attention to the beginning of each month and using it as a personal reset. It is not surprising that many of the goal-focused planners out there (Commit30, PowerSheets, and Full Focus Planner are some popular ones!) provide space to track habits over a thirty-day span and encourage goal reevaluation at monthly intervals. However, it's hard to harness the power of this fresh start if you don't notice it! Therefore, I encourage having rituals to emphasize this demarcation throughout the year.

One key strategy for this kind of emphasis is quite basic, but it definitely helps: I change my phone screen background the night before each new month starts! There are plenty of free seasonal screen backgrounds available for your electronic device if you search, and many of them will incorporate the current month's name, calendar, and overall vibe. I change both my home and lock screens, and absolutely love waking up on September 1 and seeing a barrel of apples instead of the beach picture that marked August (and that I probably stopped noticing a few weeks prior).

If you prefer backgrounds featuring your own family members, you can still choose pictures with seasonal elements (ski photos for January; a past Halloween shot for October). Or you could go entirely abstract and minimalist and just choose a seasonal color! Whatever your aesthetic preference is, it's fun and helpful to mark the start of the month in this simple way.

In addition to your tech, you can choose to create little "new month" reminders around your home or workspace. This can be as simple as flipping the page of a monthly calendar, using a new color scheme in your planner, or refreshing your office snack stash with seasonal selections. Monthly fresh flowers would be lot of fun for a reasonable cost outlay, and a monthly pedicure would be divine—you could perhaps schedule the appointment at the end of each month and use this ritual to celebrate wins and welcome your next four-week era.

Other Monthly Cycles That May Apply

When you hear "monthly cycle," you may not be thinking about pedicures and screen backgrounds, particularly if you are a woman of childbearing age (or have a child of your own in this category!). Yes, the monthly hormonal fluctuations that go along with menstruation deserve a mention in this chapter, too! This certainly isn't a factor for everyone, and many things can influence the ways in which our hormones influence our mood, energy, and overall capacity. But it is worth learning about, especially if you find that there is a correlation for you, personally. For specific recommendations tied to various phases in the menstrual cycle, Kendra Adachi offers a lot of wisdom and validation in her time management book *The Plan*, and another excellent resource for how to work with and not against these fluctuations is *Period Power* by Maisie Hill.

Personally, I've found that awareness is key! During my luteal phase, I often notice myself feeling more impatient, snappier, or on edge. But more than anything, simply recognizing this pattern allows me to be gentler with myself. I may not give myself a lighter schedule for those weeks specifically, but I can extend myself more kindness in the moment when I do need it around those times.

Monthly Goal Setting

Just like at the seasonal and annual level, the month provides a natural check-in point for goal setting—the monthly level is just below seasonal in the nested goals hierarchy! Similar to the levels above it, it is worth your time and effort to sit down, take stock, and do some reflection and goal generation. However, you won't need multiple hours for this session, as you likely did for the higher levels, especially annual! The idea is for your planning sessions to be proportional to the time horizon they are linked to; your monthly session can probably be finished in under two hours, depending on which "wild card" elements you add onto your core goal setting.

I often get questions about the specific timing. "What if your month and season start at the same time?" is a common quandary, as is, "What if the first of the month falls on a weekend?" You might choose to piggyback your monthly planning onto your seasonal session, if that applies, or you could do it on a separate date a few days early or even a few days into the month. Like with most aspects of planning, don't get too precious or rigid—you can choose whatever time slot works best for you! There is no prize for doing things exactly "right" (and "right" might vary from person to person anyway!). The key is actually choosing a slot and putting it into the calendar.

Once you've chosen your slot, the actual planning session will be familiar! You will begin by getting out your seasonal list (one time horizon above the month). You can start by celebrating any wins that have already happened, and then explore the remaining goals on the list. Before making any commitments, though, you will review your upcoming calendar.

When you did this exercise at the yearly level, the calendar was probably pretty empty. There were some really big things present at certain points, but if you were wondering what was in store specifically for October 17, you probably wouldn't have been able to come up with much.

At the monthly level, though, your schedule has probably started to solidify. You will be able to scan the next four to five weeks and get an accurate sense of how busy you are going to be, the big events coming up, and even medium-sized obligations on the horizon. Then, once you've completed this (fairly information-rich!) scan, you can integrate your seasonal goals list with the upcoming calendar landscape, identify your domains or categories, add a dash of holistic "what just feels right for me this month?", and generate a list of goals for your month.

On this shorter time horizon, you may find that some of the items are sounding less like big life dreams and more like tasks. Not only is that okay, but it's completely appropriate! As you travel down the time horizon hierarchy, big overwhelming projects tend to get broken down. There are times when this takes a more directed effort (more on that to come), but this will often happen organically.

Let's use a renovation project (admittedly one of my least favorite things) as an example. You might have had "renovate kitchen" on your annual list. Over the summer, you may have decided to focus on the appliances, and then in reviewing your seasonal list you recognize that July is a great time to order the new dishwasher you had been eyeing. "Order dishwasher" definitely sounds more like a task, but it is being done in service of a larger goal, and one that hasn't been forgotten—it still remains there on your seasonal list, ready for you to select another element to focus on, perhaps over the next month.

Similar to the higher levels (annual, seasonal), you need to make a strategic choice about where this monthly list will live. One easy option is to put it in the same place you have your other lists! However, some people find that lower-level lists are best placed somewhere where they can easily remain top of mind. You might choose to print out your monthly list and hang it on your wall above your desk, or it might be included on a dedicated page of your paper planner—many brands have some kind of a monthly "dashboard," which works very well for this purpose. Digital solutions work well here, too, if you like to file your goals as a digital note or via an app like Trello, Todoist, or Notion.

Habit Streaks and the "Twenty-One Days" Myth

Some of the goals we may choose to set are habit goals. We've all heard the saying that "twenty-one days is a habit"—but where did this adage come from, and is it actually true? If you've successfully stuck to your new habit goal for the better part of a month, can you relax and assume you're done with work in this area?

After hearing this figure thrown around nonchalantly for decades, I was surprised to find out that it was based on…well, not very much! Plastic surgeon Maxwell Maltz wrote a self-help book in 1960 titled *Psycho-Cybernetics,* and in this book, he noted that it often took his patients twenty-one days to get used to their new surgically altered appearances.[2] This was not quantified in any official manner, and the idea that this extended to habit formation was pure extrapolation. In other words, it was a theory based on an idea applied to a very specific context. This is not typically how the scientific method works, but it was catchy and interesting and probably caught on for those reasons.

There has been some research on how long it takes for certain learned behaviors to become automatic, though. One of the most famous is a 2009 study on habit formation that looked at that adaptation of a "drinking or activity behavior to carry out daily in the same context."[3] The overarching conclusion here regarding the time it takes to form a habit was essentially "it varies," as depending on the subject and context the length of time ranged between 18 and 254 days—quite a spread! Sadly, this much less memorable result failed to resonate in the same way that twenty-one days did, and thus the myth still stands.

Does this mean that setting habit goals for a thirty-day period is worthless? In my opinion, no! But it may mean that many habits will take more than one month to become sticky, and this might allow you to be more open minded about what constitutes success.

Monthly Adventures and Fun Lists

Seasonal bucket lists are fairly common. Social media gets saturated with summer fun lists around the start of June, and there are seasonal equivalents for winter, spring, fall, and the holiday season. However, I hope to convince you to zoom in with your fun lists and consider creating them for each month.

The main benefit to the month as a time frame for these kinds of lists is that the month tends to be the level where ideas go from theoretical "that sounds fun!" exclamations to actual calendar items. The monthly level is where you can actually see that there are two free weekends, because the other two contain a soccer tournament and a work trip. The month does contain enough time to make plans—from a purely practical standpoint, if you relegate your fun lists to a weekly (or daily!) level, you might have trouble booking that reservation or obtaining childcare.

The month is also long enough that having a few fun activities planned hits the sweet spots of *specialness*. By this, I mean that the events aren't happening every single day (because how special would that really feel?), but they also aren't so rare that they feel super high stakes or have little impact on your overall life experience.

What does this monthly fun look like? Well, just like with your goals and priorities, you get to decide! That said, I know sometimes coming up with ideas (even fun ones) out of thin air can feel daunting. So, here are some potential angles to consider:

- **One multiday experience per month that you are excited about.** This doesn't have to involve travel, though it certainly can! Perhaps you will dedicate a weekend to apples—you can celebrate the start of fall with apple picking on Saturday and tackle an apple-centric baking challenge on Sunday. Or, during a very stressful period, maybe you will have a quiet but luxurious self-care extravaganza featuring two nights' worth of home sheet masks and *Emily in Paris*.
- **A few events that are social.** These can be anything you want them to be, and they can shift with the phase of life you find yourself in. Maybe they are date nights, or perhaps you are in that hazy newborn phase and the only social events that sound

appealing or realistic are stroller walks with friends (or even with a far-flung friend on the phone).

- **Some kind of themed list or quest!** In her brilliant book *You Only Die Once*, Jodi Wellman encourages readers to create "fun lists" at any level that feels right, with examples like "Things We'll Do in the Best July Ever" and "Top 20 Ways We'll Crush Our Winter Holidays."[4] Defining your list and perhaps even choosing a slightly saucy title might help shape your vision for the month—and if nothing else, it will probably be fun to create and attempt to go through your list.

The common theme in almost all of the fun listed above? It's planning. Of course, serendipity is *possible*—you might run into a friend unexpectedly and enjoy a stroller walk together because your nap schedules are synced and you just happen to live near each other. But it's far less likely, and while serendipity tends to be romanticized, the unplanned aspect probably won't add all that much to the fun factor. By spending some time actively thinking about the fun you'd like to have and then putting some of the building blocks into place, you are likely to have more fun. Full stop. The monthly level is the perfect time horizon to bring these fun ideas firmly into reality.

Life Maintenance Tasks: Moving away from Reactivity

In addition to focusing on fun, the month is a great interval for some cyclical nuts-and-bolts life maintenance. Your needs may vary based on your current stage of life and the responsibilities on your plate, but most of us need to do some basic recurring tasks centered around our finances, our physical spaces, and our bodies (everyone eats, right?). Creating a regular process for each of these areas on a monthly basis does take time, but it can be pivotal in preventing routine tasks from reaching unnecessarily urgent status. If you've ever made a 10:00 p.m. run for hamster food, you know exactly what I'm talking about here. (A far more proactive solution is to have the seed blend that little Leif prefers shipped automatically!)

Budgeting and Bills

Money! We all have it, therefore we all have to think about it…at least some of the time. There is a very interesting culture surrounding finances in this day and age—no one likes to talk about specifics of how they spend, even though it's one of the clearest manifestations of one's values. Plus, we could probably learn a lot from seeing a variety of different budgets!

That said, the most important budget to understand is your own. As discussed in the previous chapter, for quite some time I was clueless about the specific ins and outs of our accounts as well as the big-picture aspects of our family's finances. This isn't some story about how I was letting my husband take the lead in this realm; nope, no one was steering this particular ship. We were earning and spending and nothing terrible was happening, so we didn't really stop to examine the specifics.

In addition to the seasonal finance meetings we started having (very valuable!), we started getting very granular about our earnings and expenditures, and this happened at the monthly level. The reasons for using the month as time frame for setting up our projected budget and allocating funds were simple. First, many expenses occur monthly (think electricity, mortgage, car payment). It isn't that easy for me to estimate off the top of my head how much money goes to Florida Power & Light over the course of a year, but I can definitely tell you the monthly range. Second, a month provides enough time to prevent you from feeling like you're dealing with your budget constantly—but it's frequent enough to make each session manageable. Case in point: I would be daunted by the thought of an entire season's worth of credit card statements, but a month is doable. Finally, most budgeting apps use the month as standard time frame for budgeting. This is probably due to the factors noted here, plus you can usually estimate what your income is likely to look like over the course of the month. If you work in a very unpredictable field, it's trickier, but you can get around this by essentially allocating last month's earnings to the current month's budget.

There are many ways to go about tracking your budget, but I think zero-based budgeting is incredibly powerful. With this method, you look at your take-home income for the month (after any autopilot savings and tax deductions) and put every single dollar into a budget category. Some categories will be pure spending (groceries, kid activities, and household goods, for example) and other categories will be for short-term savings (think travel, home maintenance, or emergency fund). You can include longer-term savings here, too, like multiyear fund for a new car or even a college savings plan (a 529 savings plan or other type of fund).

In defining your categories each month and tracking your expenses, you will gain an awareness of how well your spending patterns reflect your values and your intentions. We have used the information from this practice to help us with life decisions both big and small, such as determining whether to get a new car or fix up our thirteen-year-old Prius (we went with the latter) and figuring out where it makes the most sense to shop for groceries.

To put this method into place, you can use an app that has automatic categorization of your various expenses, you can create your own DIY version using a spreadsheet, or you can find something between these levels of automation. Personally, I prefer the middle-ground approach, using a popular app (You Need a Budget) to organize my monthly expenditures. This app is easy to use on the fly and automates a lot of the math, but we enter in much of the data ourselves and audit it on a monthly basis, generally on the first weekend of the month. I wholeheartedly believe that this practice and the awareness it has brought to our spending habits has helped us save more strategically—and perhaps just as importantly, spend out on the things we truly value. Unlike time, money is replaceable, but it's still a limited resource for almost all of us and in some cases can even be used to *buy* time! So intentional stewardship of our financial lives is an important piece of the planning puzzle.

On that note, there are probably a few of you who are now shaking your heads and wondering why all of this work (and it is work!) is necessary. You may be right! I have friends who are truly not spenders, and if you are in this category, creating and auditing your monthly budget may not be for you! One particularly frugal friend has said to me, "We live so far below our means that tracking just isn't worth our time." Instead, she focuses on the long view, and if she sees their savings growing nicely, she assumes that all is well. She happens to work in finance, so she knows what she's talking about. I believe it, and I'm slightly jealous! But for those of us more prone to impulse buys or lifestyle inflation, this practice is incredibly revealing and helpful.

Paper Cleanup

It would be wonderful to live in a paperless society, but it doesn't seem like we're there yet, judging from the numerous sheets that emerge from my first grader's backpack on the regular! The overall volume of pages may be downshifting, but it definitely hasn't hit zero and may not anytime soon. Furthermore, some of the things that we receive on paper are things that we do need to keep around, though sometimes a digital version will suffice!

If you tend to be an accumulator of piles on your desk (I will sheepishly raise my own hand as a member of this group!), monthly is a great interval to consider a cleanup. This way, you can let things sit out in the open for a bit, but you'll never accumulate to the point of disaster. In these clear-the-decks sessions, you can choose to save things digitally in your preferred system, or you can go old-school with a traditional filing cabinet. Even more ideas for organizing paper can be found in Lisa Woodruff's excellent and practical book, *The Paper Solution.* Notably, even your paper receptacles (tangible or digital) benefit from regular editing, but for these, yearly is probably reasonable!

Decluttering

I absolutely loved *The Life-Changing Magic of Tidying Up* by Marie Kondo and adore the idea of having a home filled with only things I use or love. However, my actual surroundings do not reflect these ideals—chalk it up to entropy or the current phase of life with three active kids!

At the same time, it could be worse. And one thing saving us from reaching a dangerous level of clutter is some practice of regular pruning, often done in categories. I absolutely have not reached decluttering peace here, and in a way I feel a bit ridiculous writing this chapter from my office/closet, because at this very moment, last year's Halloween costume, an old half marathon medal, and a handbag I haven't picked up since 2015 are all within my line of sight. However, the most successful I have ever been with decluttering was the year I decided to choose a room each month and check it off as the year progressed. I think there is something to the idea that even twelve days of curating your belongings over a 365-day year can make a significant dent, especially if performed in a strategic pattern.

One method would be to choose twelve categories of items, which is Marie Kondo–inspired: books, personal belongings, sentimental items, clothing, and the like. Another method (perhaps more suited to those of us with multiple rooms filled with stuff) would be to go by room: kitchen, then bathroom, then bedroom, and so on.

Two to three hours spent in each space or in each category would absolutely not lead to organizational bliss and Pinterest-perfect images of shelves filled with sparse goods arranged by color. But it would certainly get you farther than having no regular ritual at all! I like the idea of setting this up on a monthly cadence, but depending on your situation this could also be seasonal or even weekly, if you're in an intense season of home improvement.

Meal Planning

I know what you're thinking: *Don't most people plan meals out on a weekly basis?* Yes. And we will definitely return to this topic in the next chapter! But more broadly, the month can be a helpful lens to look at household operations around food. Devoting just a few minutes to think about the upcoming month of meals could open up a few opportunities.

First, you can make a concerted effort to think about what you already have on hand, so you can make plans to use it up! If you have a freezer stash, looking at this at the start of the month might allow you to find the perfect night over the next few weeks to use up that lasagna—and one hack I love is to actually add the task of taking the meal out to thaw to your calendar. Thinking ahead a full month will also allow you to take better advantage of bulk deals, as you might envision several uses for one ingredient over the course of the month. If you tend to order takeout, making a list of places you really want to try over the next month might help you come up with fresh options when you're already tired and hungry. Finally, if you're in a major meal-planning rut, try choosing a cookbook to cook out of for the entire month! This will force you into trying some new recipes and will remove some of the decision fatigue many of us have around meal planning.

Household Supply Blitz

Not having what you need in the moment is the worst. Toilet paper! Baking powder! Hamster food! (As previously mentioned, this is not a good item to run out of.) Running out of household necessities turns a mundane and easy task into a mini-emergency. One of my course attendees recently bemoaned the fact that her day care often tells her that they need a fresh economy-sized box of diapers at the last possible moment. This doesn't sound like a big deal, yet it forces her into reactive problem-solving mode at a time when maybe she just wants to get home, eat dinner, put the baby to bed, clean up, and enjoy the twenty minutes of relaxation and Netflix she had been looking forward to all day. It seems like such a small thing, but in the moment, it's incredibly frustrating!

The best way to prevent these reactivity bombs from going off is to get ahead of them. And the best way to accomplish that is a regular routine of auditing your current stashes and making sure to replenish them! There are some items where a monthly cadence for doing this would not make sense—you're not going to buy twenty gallons of milk and audit this collection in your fridge monthly. But for many nonperishable household goods, a month can be perfect. If you always make sure you have a month's worth of stuff and you take the time to check in on your supplies every month, you should be golden. Will there still be "urgent" trips to the grocery store because a school project requires a very specific brand of pasta for the kids to make noodle-based bridges in physics? Yes, this will happen (or at least it has to me). But even reducing the frequency of these eleventh-hour "I need it now!" events is a major step in moving from reactivity to proactivity!

Prescriptions and subscriptions fall into this category as well. Medicines can be particularly hard to source sometimes, so ensuring you navigate the landscape of refill requests and pharmacy availability on a regular basis can be (literally) lifesaving. Subscriptions are great and can save both money and time, but sometimes they have to be actively managed. I know that I had better look at my subscriptions each month and cancel what I don't need, or I'll end up with a stockpile of all the wrong things. This is therefore a part of my monthly review process that I never miss.

Errands and Appointments

The start of a month is a useful point to look at your upcoming appointments: both those that are already scheduled as well as ones that haven't gotten made yet. Your schedule is defined enough that you can make effective choices about where to put an upcoming nail salon visit, but things (generally) won't be so packed that you can't fit them in. (Unless it's May and you have school-age children, in which case my advice would be to just leave any nonessential appointments out for the month altogether!)

You can ensure you have no major conflicts and also slot in more flexible errands like dry cleaning, hair maintenance, or pet grooming. One caveat is that certain medical specialties require booking far in advance of one month, but you can at least check in monthly to ensure your future sessions are set for the foreseeable future.

Putting it all together, this chapter provides a framework for monthly planning and goal setting, plus suggestions for monthly life maintenance rituals in several realms. Up next, we'll move down another time horizon to tackle the week!

Monthly Planning Checklist

☐ Consider ways to mark the start of the month.

- Ideas: new phone screen, fresh flowers, monthly photo calendar, or new color scheme

☐ Set monthly goals.

- Review seasonal goals list.
- Review last month's goals, celebrate wins, and choose what, if anything, to migrate to the current month.
- Review the upcoming calendar landscape.
- Holistic self-assessment: consider how you feel and what seems to fit the overall vibe or mood of the upcoming month.
- Create your month's goals list in domains.

☐ Go beyond goals.

- Consider your habits and decide if there are any that make sense to focus on or track this month.
- Audit the upcoming month for fun and connection!

☐ Monthly life maintenance tasks: choose any that apply!

- Budgeting and bills
- Paper management
- Decluttering
- Meal planning
- Household supply blitz
- Errands and appointments

☐ Book your next monthly planning session on the calendar!

The Week

Playing Time Tetris with Your 168 Hours

Yes, we are zooming in once again! Full disclosure: the week is my absolute favorite time horizon to think about. All of them are important, but if you were going to work on mastering your planning at just one level to start with, I would tell you to go with the week. When I miss out on my own weekly planning rituals (hey, even planning aficionados get behind sometimes!), I feel much more stress, and I don't enjoy my Mondays the way I do when I am ready for them. In an unplanned week, I am far less likely to fit in fun activities or carve out time to focus on my highest priorities. These off weeks expose just how important weekly planning is for me, and in the end, I emerge determined to get back into my usual planning rhythms since I can see what a difference they make.

A week feels both expansive and manageable. Your week likely contains multitudes, and yet it's short enough that you have a fairly good understanding of what it will look and feel like at the start of each fresh seven-day stretch. One hundred sixty-eight hours is enough time to have a variety of experiences, exist in a whole bunch of different contexts, and get quite a bit done (or not, depending on the kind of week it happens to be). Over the course of a recent week, I worked three days in clinic, navigated a new and somewhat stressful parenting challenge, recorded two podcast episodes, followed my workout schedule, and saw Taylor Swift in concert (well, it just happened to be an incredibly great week!). I also drove a lot (kids and myself), sent many emails, and did sundry household tasks ranging from bill paying to kid lunch prep to buying groceries and beyond. It is amazing how much fits into 168 hours, and I know I am not some wild outlier. If you are reading this, I suspect you have plenty of different things packed into your weeks, too.

Some activities are exciting and fun, while others are mundane but necessary. Together, they fill each seven-day cycle that, repeated endlessly, forms the rhythm of your life. Strategizing and planning will enable you to make informed decisions about what fits and what doesn't and to proactively pave the road ahead so that you can be present for the actual things you will be doing.

I have two major sources of inspiration when it comes to thinking about the week. One is David Allen, author of *Getting Things Done*. He is a childfree man in his late seventies, and his iconic time-management manual made a huge impact on many (including me!) when it came out in 2001. The other is Laura Vanderkam, author of *168 Hours* and *Tranquility by Tuesday*, among many other great books about time. Laura is a mother of five and has been writing about time since her early years of motherhood. Laura has since become a close friend and colleague of mine (we have recorded hundreds of podcast episodes together to date!), but before I knew her personally, I was blown away by her perspectives on the week as a unit of time.

From David Allen, I learned all about the power of the weekly review, his term for a structured check-in held at weekly intervals designed to help you clear the decks and prepare for the week to come. This concept is actually one of the main inspirations for the nested goals system—after all, if you can have a weekly review, why not monthly, seasonal, and yearly reviews? Therefore, this practice is going to seem familiar, though at the weekly level there are a few twists as things get a bit more granular and specific compared to planning at the larger time horizons. From Laura Vanderkam, I learned just how much can fit in a well-orchestrated week, the importance of thinking through weekly operations, and how the choices we make around weekly routines (the seemingly mundane things we do over and over again each week) are incredibly important, as they shape the fabric of our lives. The custom weekly planning process detailed below incorporates elements I have learned from each of these experts, from the structured review components to ensuring all of the pieces fit while building in time for fun and personal growth.

Your Custom Weekly Review

The classic weekly review from *Getting Things Done* has three components: (1) get clear (process all lingering loose ends and inboxes); (2) get current (review your various lists and active projects); and (3) get creative (decide what, if anything, you'd like to add to your lists).[1] I cannot underestimate the power of this practice and how much it has impacted my life. However, I think that many of us can get even more personal about what kinds of things belong in our own versions of the weekly review, so I recommend taking this practice one step further and customizing it. There are some items that are going to be important for everyone (these are core nested goals practices, so they will be familiar!) and some that will be very individualized. You can imagine that a new mother heading back to work likely has very different preparation needs from a retiree or a twentysomething graduate student.

Let's start with the basics that everyone will need to include:

Weekly Planning Part 1: Reflection and Review

Parallel to the larger time horizons (annual/seasonal/monthly), your planning process begins with an overview of the prior week. At each level, your focus is going to be less dreamy and more practical. You're noting what got accomplished last week and what didn't, so you can decide what to carry forward into the next seven-day time frame. Take a moment to celebrate even small wins, as we often skate past our accomplishments. Then, try to keep your attitude neutral and exploratory as you scan for unchecked boxes and loose ends. For each of these, there are several options:

- **Migrate it to the next week's list.** This is probably the most common fate of an undone task at the weekly level, and is pretty straightforward—you're just moving it to the next week's list of tasks.
- **Assign it a specific time slot.** Sometimes deadlines start to

loom once a task gets migrated once or twice and therefore now commands a higher degree of urgency. In this case, it might make more sense to simply turn your task into a time-specific item and place it directly on your master calendar.

- **Make it more specific.** As into planning as I am, even I sometimes put things on my weekly list that have no business being there. Think "taxes." Or "plan summer trip." It's not a shock that behemoth projects like these end up untouched by the end of the week—these are multistep projects rather than tasks, and therefore having them in this context is intimidating and incredibly unappealing. Can you imagine having fifteen free minutes in the carpool line and thinking, *Hey, I think I'll pay my taxes now!*? This is a weekly list, and the scope of each item must be scaled accordingly. Identify the next step—perhaps it's to buy 1099 forms, to update your expenses spreadsheet, or to email your accountant to set up a meeting—and shrink this task so that you won't recoil in horror next week when you see it on your list.
- **Delegate it.** Sometimes I will notice a task moving forward time and time again, and it's not because it's too big—it's just that I really don't want to do it! It's not always feasible, but many times there is some form of asking for help that could be considered. You can pay a professional, ask a friend, or discuss it with your partner. Delegation certainly applies in the work context, but it doesn't have to mean a formal business agreement. I often delegate birthday party invitation duties to my teen, since she's better at creating themed graphics than

I am! If you do choose this option, it can be very helpful to leave yourself a reminder to follow up on what was delegated. My favorite way to do this is to simply add a reminder note to a future calendar date, or you can also create a "waiting-for" list (yet another David Allen recommendation!), which is a collection of pending items that gets reviewed on a regular basis.

- **Let it go!** Just because it went on your list at one point in time does not mean you actually have to do it. This is obvious to some, but not to everyone—admittedly, including me. There *may* be consequences to crossing something off your list, but there also may not be, or perhaps those consequences are just worth it. Using the examples above, I would not recommend moving on from "pay taxes" with a shrug, but perhaps you can just table planning that summer trip for now! Maybe inspiration will hit closer to summer and you'll have a serendipitous adventure, or you'll enjoy a staycation.

Once you've reviewed the prior week, it's time to look at the time frame directly above the week in the nested goals hierarchy: the month! Get out your monthly list and review the items you listed on there. This may be a fresh list, if the week in question begins near the start of a month, or it may be up to four weeks old by this point. Mark it up if you'd like, noting anything that might fit or feels relevant to the week ahead. You're not at the commitment stage yet, but it's great to have these ideas fresh in your mind as you go through the steps toward generating this week's goals.

Weekly Planning Part 2: Look ahead to Avoid Trouble

It's time to review your calendar landscape. However, you'll notice the view getting a lot clearer and more detailed from this vantage point! Things on your master calendar are now at the point where they are far from theoretical. They are *happening*, unless something really wild happens (and it still might, but it probably won't).

Therefore, you want your master calendar overview at the weekly level to be careful and complete. Don't just do a broad overview; instead, take a few moments to go through day by day, envisioning what it would be like to navigate your upcoming week as it is currently slated. Look for conflicts, too-short transitions, or an overloaded day. Sometimes tight scheduling is unavoidable, but if you know where the trickiest spots are, you may be able to make a few strategic changes. At the very least, you'll be prepared and aware enough to avoid adding on to a particularly hectic stretch.

As for completeness, it never hurts do to a brief audit of all of your usual suspects for calendar subterfuge: Outlook meetings plunked down from above, late-breaking soccer app notifications, and the like. You can never be 100 percent sure that you've seen everything, but most people get a sense of where the sneakiest schedule changes tend to hide.

Weekly Planning Part 3: Look Around

Okay, here's a key point: in order to really be sure what is on your plate as you plan your upcoming week, you have to be up-to-date with all of the places where tasks and obligations lurk. This part is not nearly as fun as looking at your nested goals lists. No one likes the idea of spending their limited planning time cleaning out their inboxes!

Inbox processing (for any type of inbox!) is addressed in chapter 1, but the specific timing for this process wasn't addressed. I try to avoid being overly prescriptive, but I'm going to make a recommendation anyway: I think most people benefit from completing a "full processing" cycle every week, right before or as part of their weekly planning process.

I know. It isn't fun, it isn't sexy, and it will make the weekly planning process less of a breeze. But if you don't take the time to get a full picture of what kinds of tasks and requests are out there waiting for you, you may find out much too late, when "proactive" has left the building days ago, and it's impossible to order that random-but-incredibly-crucial-school-project-thing online. I'm not necessarily saying you need to do an epic "from 28,583 emails to 0" cleanout within your planning session, but you should ensure you are as close to up-to-date as you can be when you start to plan. This may mean that you do mini-inbox excavations on Monday, Wednesday, and Friday, with the last one right before your planning session.

Weekly Planning Part 4: Look Within

Taking stock of your mood and energy is helpful at every level, but this analysis becomes even more important and actionable when applied to smaller time frames. In truth, it's not always easy to identify one dominant vibe for an entire season. You may have extremely high energy for one part and feel like hibernating for the rest. A week, though, is much shorter, so you may have more accurate ideas about your impending hormonal milieu, sleep debt, or mental state. As noted in the last chapter, I personally tend to suffer from lower moods (translation:

a lot of tears, very little patience) before each menstrual cycle, and I will absolutely know going into a week if this will be a factor in my capacity. Or maybe someone in our household just got sick, and I'm awaiting the inevitable spread among the rest of us. The step of looking within is important, as it helps to ensure the week you're about to set up for yourself is created with a realistic perspective and appropriate self-compassion.

Weekly Planning Part 5: Generate Weekly Tasks

If you've completed steps 1 through 4, you are primed, prepped, and ready. You will probably have a great deal of clarity around what kind of week you're headed into, what feels most urgent, and what you'd like to get done. Capture the essential items on a list, and if it helps, organize them by category or domain. I often have just two categories separating my weekly list: "work" and "home," as almost all of my weekly tasks fit one of these domains. You can color code or separate the weekly list into two. Ideally, your weekly list will contain no more than fifteen items. If you've identified even more than that, you may want to consider consolidating some of them (perhaps "buy soap" "buy detergent" and "buy sponges" becomes "cleaning supplies: soap, detergent, sponges"). You may also consider scheduling them directly. If you have to meet with each of your eight team members, these can exist as calendar items and won't need to take up space on your weekly list. Very long lists become unwieldy and intimidating and won't be as useful when you're referring to your weekly list to plan your day (which is the part that actually leads to things getting accomplished!).

In the courses I have taught, participants are always eager to hear exactly where I keep my weekly lists or where I recommend they should be kept. Really, this is an individual choice! These task lists can exist anywhere as long as it's a place you will be referring to often (generally at least daily). For me, the most convenient location is directly in my paper planner, listed in a column to the left of my vertical weekly layout. But you may not enjoy this configuration, or perhaps you plan only in the digital space. That's completely reasonable and will work just as well!

If you do plan digitally, you can create lists in most task management apps that you label with the dates in your week. (These change from year to year, but Google Tasks, Todoist, Wonderlist, and Trello are a few that have been around for some time now.) You could also capture and organize your lists in a note-taking app like Apple Notes or Notion.

If you don't use a paper planner but want to plan using other analog tools, a bullet journal can be a great place for weekly task collection. Invented by Ryder Carroll, the bullet journal is an open-ended and flexible planning system typically contained in a dot grid notebook. For those who mostly stay in one place, a giant dry-erase board can be a great place to keep your weekly list of tasks. (If nothing else, it's extra satisfying to check things off on a giant whiteboard!)

One advantage to a more traditional paper planner is that a planner that spans a year has many future weekly lists already available for you; this can be helpful when things come up that are tied to a future time frame but not necessarily a particular day. To some degree, this can be simulated in the digital space by adding your task to a future date to address later, but it's less straightforward (in most apps, at least) to pin a task to a future week.

Choose tools that you enjoy—perhaps something that feels nice in hand or has a design that is calming to you—and focus on the habit of creating and referencing your list. The magic is in the method, not the materials.

Add Weekly Operations for Smooth(er) Sailing

Your nested goals practice is one important piece of the weekly planning puzzle, but for many people the review process does not end with the creation of a task list. You likely also have some other things you need to have set. Here, I'll refer to them as "weekly ops."

Picture yourself on a busy Monday morning. You're heading into a packed work week, and you've already reviewed your hard landscape (firmly scheduled commitments already on the calendar) and created a really- well-thought-out list of tasks you'd like to accomplish. But...do you know what you'll be wearing?

Some people (like me) couldn't care less about this particular weekly operations element! I don't really think about my outfits in advance unless I'm packing for a trip (and even then, sometimes I just wing it). But for someone else, this preparation might feel essential. For most of us, there are probably at least a few additional planning elements that help us feel truly ready and prepared to dive into another 168-hour cycle. These things won't be the same for every individual, so this is where your weekly review starts to become customized. In this section, I'll provide a number of ideas for these personalized selections. I definitely do not recommend throwing every suggestion into your weekly preparation routine; personally, I include only three of the below options (meal planning, kid logistics, and movement). Choose the ones that you find really provide a feeling of readiness, and feel free to experiment—you can always add or subtract down the line!

Wardrobe

As I mentioned, I do not include this in my own weekly ops; most days you can find me in either scrubs (in a rotating cast of colors!) or jeans and a T-shirt. But perhaps you love fashion, or maybe you don't but you have a corporate role where your outfits really matter! I have one friend who practices at a high-end law firm in Texas, and not only does she have a personal stylist, but she plans her outfits out in advance. If you have a hectic morning routine and your look requires matching items and a more-than-negligible amount of dry cleaning, planning your outfits for the week makes sense. My own teen has been known to prepare five days of school gear in a hanging organizer, though now she wears a school uniform which has significantly reduced her sartorial mental load!

Meals

Well, this could be an entire book. And, in fact, it is! There are some amazing books on meal planning—Kendra Adachi's *The Lazy Genius Kitchen* comes to mind as a really great guide on this topic. That said, it still deserves mention here because I am fairly sure I am not alone in feeling like heading into Monday without an idea of what we are going to eat for dinner feels almost…reckless. Meal planning is an essential weekly ops item for me. Notably, these ops elements do not need to be performed all at once or even at the same time you create your goals.

My meal planning usually happens on Sundays, because this tends to be when I like to shop (though sometimes the crowds at Trader Joe's make me think I should consider a new approach).

In our house, meal planning weekly ops also includes some consideration of lunches and snacks (do we have some options for the kids?) and a general audit of the fridge and pantry contents.

I include some of this meal planning information directly in my planner within the weekly spread; it fits near the bottom of the vertical columns, taking up space that otherwise would have been used for scheduling activities after 10:00 p.m. (of which there are none, because I'm too tired!). However, this is just one of many options. You could use a whiteboard, a piece of paper stuck on the fridge with a clip, a separate meal planning notebook, or your electronic resource of choice.

Movement

I recognize that this is an acquired taste, but I used to enjoy training for marathons (I don't do that anymore, but that could be the subject of a whole other book!). Running higher mileage has been a very off-and-on endeavor for me depending on the ages of my kids and a host of health factors. But I still love to exercise most days, and I always include a plan for my workouts in my weekly ops! Putting my planned fitness classes and strength training sessions directly in my planner helps me to see where they fit (or don't fit, as the case may be). If you exercise regularly, it can be helpful to plan this out on a weekly basis.

If that sounds incredibly distasteful to you, you may be a more rebellious type. As an aside, Gretchen Rubin coined the term "Rebel" for people who respond to neither outer nor inner expectations, and it's a useful thing to know about oneself.[2] If you are the kind of person who has little interest in scheduling workouts, definitely feel free to skip this one. Maybe you could mark the days you had some movement in there after the fact (or not!).

Sleep

This sounds odd, but hear me out: There may be circumstances when it makes sense to think about sleep on a weekly basis. Some people have shift work and need to strategize around naps during the day. Others may be battling an illness that impacts sleep. Some may have babies who love to eat at midnight and then wake up at the very first photon of light at dawn (so cute in their sleep sacks but also so alarmingly EARLY). If sleep deprivation is an issue for you, looking at your week to figure out where you might be able to sleep in or make up for a deficit can be helpful. Perhaps you could identify some strategic windows to catch a nap or discuss some early-morning-wake-up trades with a partner. If you already have a fixed routine each week, this might not be necessary (I love to sleep a little bit longer on Sunday!), but if things are a bit less standardized, including this element in your weekly ops might help. Everything is harder when you are tired!

Childcare and Other Related Logistics

This is probably my most time-consuming weekly ops activity, but our household would really struggle to function well without it. As of the time of this writing, I have three children in two different schools. Between them, they have approximately 84,273 activities. There is soccer (school soccer AND club soccer, because why play on just one team?), gymnastics, piano, tutoring, dance, and more. There are multiple carpools and drivers. We have a wonderful nanny, and there are a lot of moving parts. Calendar management is a core part of the initial weekly review process, but most of the time, kid-related logistics need more attention than a cursory calendar sweep.

When the kids were younger, these ops were mostly about childcare. Out of necessity, I had to assess things like: Is anyone sick? Is anyone sort-of-starting-to-seem-like-they-might-be-getting-sick, and when will her brother catch it? Is preschool closed or is there some kind of random early release day? Do I have any later work obligations that would require care outside of standard hours?

I also thought about childcare on the weekends, if needed. In this particular category, though, I quickly learned a hack: look two to three weekends ahead, and incorporate this in my weekly planning. Babysitters are much more likely to say yes to a sitting request in a few weeks, when their own personal calendars are looking less full and hectic. Plus, date nights are such a lovely bright spot to look forward to. Not only does planning these a bit farther ahead make snagging the kids' favorite sitter more feasible, you can also enjoy the longer anticipation phase!

Now, things are a bit different. The only constant of parenting (and life, I suppose) is change! But I still enjoy date nights and other adventures. Which brings me to the next category…

Fun!

Yes, fun. One of the reasons planning sometimes gets a bad rap is that people assume that all plans must somehow relate back to optimizing efficiency, productivity, or some other metric frequently referenced in a corporate boardroom. I reject this idea!

Earlier in this chapter, I mentioned Laura Vanderkam, my podcasting partner and good friend. She is very, very serious about the concept of planning in fun. And not just family fun or some kind of enriching fun that has an ulterior motive, but also things that you simply enjoy, whether they are active, passive, social, or solitary. In her (excellent) book *Tranquility by Tuesday*, she recommends incorporating one small adventure and one larger adventure into each week.[3] Her suggested scope for a big adventure is something that might take the larger part of a day, often on the weekend. A small adventure is something that fits in a weeknight; it can be as simple as trying a new cuisine (takeout or homemade!) for Thursday night's dinner. Is it possible that some of life's adventures might just happen serendipitously? Of course! But probably not nearly as often as they would if you spent time thinking about the fun you would like to have and then put it directly on your calendar.

Other Household Care Tasks

This particular category can be a slippery slope, and I urge you to consider it carefully! For some, it's helpful to think about when you will complete various household tasks, from laundry to bathroom cleaning and beyond. Maybe you prefer to plan which days you'll do laundry so that you *don't* spend time thinking about it on other days. Others (myself included) prefer a more reactive approach to tasks in this particular realm, in part because the amount of time you could potentially devote to this area of life is limitless, and we have that whole FUN category already planned, remember!?

Neither approach is the "right" one, but make sure you know yourself before you start listing five chores for each day when you know you will take one look at those assignments and consider throwing your planner out the window.

Another side note is that if you tend to do the same core household care tasks each week, you may be better off thinking about them as routines (Thursday is laundry night!) that you evaluate each season rather than isolated events you want to think about every week. But again, your mileage may vary, so I did include this category as it can be a helpful weekly ops add-in for some.

Spiritual Practices

For many people, activities associated with their church, temple, or other spiritual activities are important pillars for each week. If this is the case for you, make sure to take a few moments to ensure key meetings and events are in your calendar, and think about any related service or volunteering. If you tend to celebrate religious holidays with large gatherings that require preparation, make sure to look ahead to when these are coming up so that you can make arrangements (send invites, make plans with family, or procure special food or other related items).

Media

For some, this may naturally fall under the "fun" umbrella, but it feels worth mentioning on its own. Maybe you're a TV or movie aficionado who likes to plan your viewing in advance—or for extra fun, you could arrange a buddy-watch with a friend! If you're a sports buff, you might want to check which of your favorite teams are slated to play in the upcoming week. The information will probably reach you anyway (my husband seems to know the Miami Heat and Duke Basketball schedules by osmosis), but this way you can look forward to the event, make space for it in your calendar, and stock up on your favorite snacks, if desired.

Financial Audit

This can be a useful weekly practice if your budget is tight (i.e., you need to make sure you have enough cash on hand to pay your bills) or if you feel overwhelmed looking at a month's worth of financial data at a time. Looking back just seven days, a glance through bank and credit card statements may help you see patterns or catch errors (or fraud!), and it will be much easier than going back thirty days because transactions will be fresh in your mind. (In contrast, try remembering what that apple.com line item from twenty-seven days ago was!)

Weekends

Weekends are part of the week, of course. They warrant discussion here because some people have complicated feelings about planning their weekends. Maybe they are dreamily remembering lazy Sundays in their twenties spent sleeping in and going for three-hour brunches without a single hard landscape feature in sight. If you currently enjoy this sort of lifestyle or have another set of weekend routines that make you happy, I'm not here to convince you to leave them behind. But most of us benefit as much (or more!) from planning our weekends as we do from planning out the work week. And also, if you really want the best brunch, you'll need a reservation.

So, for most of us, it's important to remember to include your weekend as you complete the steps of your weekly planning process! You certainly don't have to schedule every minute, but it can be nice to have some idea of what will take up the lion's share of your time and energy. Currently, many of our weekends revolve around various kid sports events; this means that on nontournament weekends it can be great to plan in a visit to a local attraction or plan that farther-flung shopping trip. As mentioned in the childcare section, it can be helpful to look at your upcoming weekend but also the next two or three while you're at it. This will give you enough lead time to ask friends about meeting up or, yes, make that coveted brunch reservation. You don't want to overdo it; I absolutely recognize that everyone benefits from unscheduled downtime. You can aim to strike a balance and, for many things, you can always cancel or reschedule if you need to.

Weekly Communication Plan

You've reached the final frontier of the weekly planning process, but you won't want to skip this part, particularly if you live with or coordinate your life with anyone else. You've done all of this amazing planning, but what about the other people that may be impacted by your plans? Enter the weekly communication plan!

The aim of your weekly communication plan is to make sure

everyone knows the relevant goings-on occurring over the next ~seven days. This will allow them to prepare, ask questions, note possible discrepancies with their own calendars, and generally participate in the planning process.

There are two necessary elements in any weekly communication plan: a verbal discussion and a written record. The discussion portion is key, because if there are multiple stakeholders, there should be some degree of back-and-forth expected before plans are finalized. This won't be easy to achieve if you are unilaterally sending an email or text. You might *start* with a written summary, but then everyone needs a moment to weigh in.

On the flip side, the written portion is also really essential as you want everyone to be able to reference the plan; this will also prevent "... but I thought you said you were picking up the kids!" sorts of mishaps. I have noticed the written aspect is particularly valuable for kids; they like having something to anchor to throughout the week.

The actual form of these verbal and written components may vary. We tend to have our discussion of the week's plan at dinner on Sunday. Ideally, this gives everyone a chance to weigh in and add pertinent notes. (Such as: "MOM, I need a dress for that performance on Saturday, when can we shop?!") Then our written record is on a whiteboard that has a space for each day of the week and an area for notes. This is definitely low tech, but it is also low friction and easy to change when needed. I do snap a picture of the whiteboard as it stands on Sundays and send it to my husband and our nanny (and pretty soon, I will probably include the kids). Another very popular option is to use a shared electronic calendar (Google or Apple, among others); this works well if everyone involved has their own device and uses these apps already. There are also some very aesthetically pleasing electronic devices that will integrate multiple digital calendars and apps, displaying the information in helpful ways; current options include the Skylight Calendar, the DAKboard, and the Hearth Display. One of my friends actually has a fridge with a Google Calendar widget—an ingenious use of space!

Logistics: When Will This Occur?

One of the biggest barriers to effectively completing the weekly planning process is to acknowledge that it takes a nontrivial amount of time and mental bandwidth. It's not a multiday retreat (that would be lovely, but probably doesn't fit the span of most people's weeks!), but it's likely a solid hour or two that belongs on your calendar rather than existing as a quick "fit-it-into-the-cracks" sort of activity. I recommend starting by designating one hour at minimum, and then you can always expand or contract the interval once you've done a few and have a better understanding of how long your own process takes.

I personally love doing my weekly planning in two stints: part one on Thursday and part two on Sunday. Part one includes my calendar audit, goal setting for the following week, and a first look at the next two weekends. Part two includes most of my weekly ops items (meals, exercise, kid-related logistics, fun) followed by our family communication rituals (discussion and whiteboard). This evolved organically and is still often changing, so don't be afraid to experiment! You can always try something different next week.

A Note on Atypical Weeks

One beautiful aspect of this system is that you do not have to be perfect. You can skip a week. You can even skip five weeks! In that case, you'd probably have to spend some time catching up, but it's doable.

I generally do not set weekly goals when we are about to head out on vacation, and I have also skipped a week or two altogether (or done an abbreviated version) when in crisis mode. You can also decide to take a break from formal planning just to take a break—you owe no one an explanation! Blank pages in your planner are not a failure, and they make excellent spaces for sketching, hand-lettering practice, or pen testing, in case you do feel compelled to use them up.

For the most part, though, I find that this ritual pays off significantly, as it allows for a much smoother and more intentional path through each week. There will absolutely still be bumps and surprises in every week, but you will be more ready to take them on if you are starting from a steady space where you have a clear understanding of what's coming as well as what you hope to accomplish and experience.

Weekly Planning Checklist

1. **Look back: Reflection and Review**
    1. Review last week's accomplishments.
    2. Note what didn't get done last week, and do one of the following:
        - Migrate it as is.
        - Assign it to a specific time slot.
        - Migrate it and make it smaller or more specific.
        - Delegate it.
        - Let it go!
    3. Review your most recent monthly list.

2. **Look ahead.** Review your upcoming calendar landscape and remember to check sneaky sources for calendar subterfuge.

3. **Look around.** Make sure your inboxes are processed to a degree that allows you to be confident in knowing what is on your plate for the next week. For some, this might mean aiming for weekly Inbox Zero around the time of your review process.

4. **Look within.** Assess your mood and your energy and get a holistic sense of how you feel about the upcoming week.

5. **Generate** your weekly tasks and record them somewhere convenient.
    1. Ideas: directly in your planner, in a separate notebook

you use to track tasks, on a whiteboard if you have one main work/living area, or in your digital app of choice.

6. **Add weekly ops** for smoother sailing. Choose the ones that apply to you, and feel free to experiment week to week until you figure out what feels essential. Options include:
    1. Wardrobe
    2. Meals
    3. Movement
    4. Sleep
    5. Childcare and related logistics
    6. Fun (please don't skip this one!)
    7. Other household care tasks
    8. Spiritual practices
    9. Media
    10. Financial Audit

7. **Remember your weekends!** They require planning attention, too; in some cases, they require more than a regular weekday.

8. **Plan for communication.** Your weekly plan needs to be communicated (and in some cases, discussed and negotiated) with all stakeholders. A discussion component and a written record are both recommended!

6

Planning Your Day with Intention (Because Every Day Counts!)

"The days are long, but the years are short" is an adage attributed most recently to Gretchen Rubin, author of *The Happiness Project* and many other works related to goal achievement and life satisfaction. In one of her most popular videos, she shares a poignant memory of taking her daughter on a city bus to school.[1] At first, it felt like an annoying chore. But one day, she had an epiphany—this daily task, like many others, was part of life and a meaningful phase of motherhood. It deserved to be savored just as much as the moments we typically consider "special," like birthdays and family trips. In fact, in some ways, these seemingly ordinary moments are even more pivotal and warrant notice because they are so frequent, yet they are still—in the grand scheme of things—entirely fleeting.

Seemingly mundane moments make up our days, and our days make up our lives. Another adage that I love is, "Every day counts." Jenny Stancampiano is a longtime old-school blogger (yes, like me!)

and an ultrarunner (less like me—I never ran more than 26.2 miles!) who posts at runnersfly.com; she also has two children in the teen/young adult phases of life and works full time as a massage therapist. She set "every day counts" as her theme for one year, and I found myself repeating her three wise words all year long.[2]

Like me, Jenny loves to set goals and challenge herself, but she noted at one point that she sometimes missed seeing the value in every single day, especially when things weren't going according to plan. Months after making her "every day counts" declaration, she had a calf issue when she was in the middle of training for a fifty-mile race and recognized that it was necessary to take a full week off from running, which is a very unpleasant thing for any ultrarunner to do, especially in the middle of a race build. Tempted to wallow in her misery and hit a sort of fast-forward button in her life, she instead wrote: "These seven unique and precious days—precious because the days are finite for all of us—count just as much as the most fun days ever."[3]

There is no fast-forward button in life, and it is best that we recognize that and embrace it…for the most part. It is true that there are very extreme cases in which I can imagine some sort of fast track to another day would be warranted, particularly if there is significant pain (physical or emotional) involved. My heart goes out to anyone to whom this applies, and I do think this is a real and valid caveat to the concept of "every day counts." However, we will set these exceptions aside for the rest of this chapter; planning during difficult times will be discussed further in the next chapter.

Each of these stories and examples serves to illustrate my main point, which is that every day is worth approaching with intention.

You've taken the time to set goals that lead to your big dreams, one level at a time, and planning at the daily level is the final step in bringing you to action. This is exciting and a key benefit of the nested goals system! But even beyond goal achievement, daily planning helps you create a plan to enjoy the hours up ahead, from incorporating small rituals you love to ensuring your aims are realistic (and therefore not overly stressful). Planning your day can also draw your attention to the moments you do look forward to, which can help you savor them as they unfold.

With that, let's get started with the elements needed for successful planning at the daily level!

The Four Essentials You Need to Plan Your Day

Essential #1: A Reliable Master Calendar

Yes, here it is again: your master calendar! A truly accurate and complete master calendar is absolutely key here. Since it happens daily, this is a streamlined planning session. Spending twenty minutes integrating various calendar sources just doesn't make sense and may bog you down past the point of no return. That said, it is possible that you will need to do a few last-minute checks, though—we will cover that in the process steps below.

Essential #2: Your Weekly List

This is where the rubber meets the road. At the daily level, you are bringing your tasks—some of which may have filtered down all the way from the annual level—into reality. You're actually doing the things you set out to do, bringing your nested goals dreams into reality. This is exciting!

So yes, you need that weekly list. Don't worry—this will not be the only source of your day's tasks. Perhaps you *do* have that unfortunate twelve-back-to-back-meetings day, and in that case it may be that the only tasks you can handle are preparation for those meetings, and that is what is most essential on that particular day. But it's still very helpful to have that list to refer to every single day, as we'll discuss shortly.

Essential #3: An Understanding of Desired Routines and Habits

When you go to plan your day, it often involves assigning yourself one-off tasks and making intentional decisions about how you would like to allocate your time. Your master calendar likely shows appointments, meetings, and events—all sorts of items where others expect you to spend your time in a specific way.

What is missing, though, are two things:

1. Things you do entirely for yourself. These are often things you feel will be done in "free moments"—items that do not get a designated block, but you still want to do them. In my case, this category includes reading (usually nonfiction to start the day and fiction later on), a workout (generally done early in the morning, with a few exceptions), a ten-minute meditation, and my Spanish language practice (my progress is admittedly slow, but at least I'm trying!).

2. Routines that happen every single day. These take time—often significant chunks of time! It's because they are so expected that they seem to disappear when you think about your daily activities. Examples might include the time you spend getting ready for work, prepping meals, or getting the kids ready for school. Making these invisible tasks visible is a major component of the Bright Method, a course and set of techniques taught by former attorney Kelly Nolan.[4] By getting very specific (and honest) about the time allocated to these routines, her clients are able to make more thoughtful decisions about their time.

A realistic understanding of the habits you want to incorporate most days (or a few times per week) plus a clear-eyed view of your current routines is essential for planning your day. Without this base knowledge, you are at high risk of overscheduling and overburdening yourself or shortchanging your own self-care.

To help avoid these pitfalls, a few practices can help.

- The Ideal Week exercise discussed in chapter 3 is an excellent reality check, especially if you include time for habits and repeated routines. You will quickly find out if the puzzle pieces of time simply don't fit in the 168-hour frame of a week!
- You can try tracking your time! My podcasting partner and friend Laura Vanderkam has been tracking hers for over *ten* years now. I personally struggle to track for longer than a week or so, but it can be an incredibly helpful exercise when I'm trying to understand exactly how long it takes to drive to work with two school stops (answer = seventy minutes).

- Spend a few minutes journaling about the routines you'd like to incorporate in an "ideal day." I try to think about this every season or so, and my current "try to dos" on any given day include the aforementioned reading, language practice, and meditation, plus time spent outside and some element of music (jamming to my kids' picks on the way to school absolutely counts).

Essential #4: A Protected and Designated Time Slot to Plan

I recognize that this may sound obvious. But since this is a short process, I think it's incredibly tempting for many people to assume that it will just automatically slot in somewhere. You need about ten minutes to do your daily planning. To be fair, it might take a little bit longer when starting out (maybe fifteen minutes?), but ultimately ten should be adequate. *Surely* not every minute of the day is taken up by something so crucial that it would be hard to find ten minutes to think through and plan out the day, right?

Except that time is funny that way. There will always be something else you could be doing, and it's not really all that likely that grabbing your planner and pens will be the first thing you're excited to jump into as soon as you can, especially perhaps after the first fresh exciting days of use in January. You need to come up with a specific time slot that makes sense for your planning, and it needs to be time that is not already being taken up by something else.

In choosing this time slot, you can analyze a few factors. First, when do you feel you're most likely to be in an effective planning mindset? It's not necessarily as complex as your other tasks, but planning is one of the main forms of executive function—a set of cognitive skills that are not fully developed until young adulthood.[5] Neuroscientific evidence aside, if you've ever tried to plan something complicated when you're exhausted, you've probably found it challenging. There are probably a few night owls that would do well planning the next day right before bed, but most people need to select a time when they are relatively fresh, if not at their peak.

Next, think about when you're least likely to be interrupted. Planning your day may only take ten minutes under ideal circumstances, but if your young kids wake up at the slightest sound in the morning and your sacred morning ritual has an 85 percent chance of being interrupted less than two minutes in, you probably need to come up with a better time slot. For those who work outside the home, one effective strategy is to time your work arrival for ten to fifteen minutes earlier than your regular start time and do the planning in the office rather than at home. If the mornings are rushed but there is a bit of flexibility at the last part of the workday, a similar slot could be used in late afternoon, at the end of the day.

I personally do my own daily planning very early most days; this works since I'm a few years past that "one-tiny-noise-and-everyone's-awake" phase. I absolutely adore this quiet and contemplative start to my day, coffee beside me and a fresh daily planning page ready to be marked up. It feels natural to think about the next twenty-four hours laid out in front of me shortly after waking up, but it is not the only time slot that works. If you are first starting out, whatever the time you choose, I highly encourage you to schedule it like you would a doctor's appointment or a work meeting; add it to your digital or paper calendar and think of it as a real event that takes up time. Eventually you will settle into a routine and won't need to do this, but I think it really can help bring this practice from an aspirational sort of idea into your daily lived reality.

To briefly recap, for daily planning you need four things: a reliable master calendar, a weekly task list, an understanding of your daily routines and desired habits, and a designated time slot to conduct this practice.

So, what do these ten minutes look like? Similar to the planning rituals at every time horizon! But a much briefer version, plus this round is perhaps the most exciting and pivotal, as you're putting tasks on your list to be done that very day.

Steps for Daily Planning: Ten Minutes to a More Proactive and Peaceful Day

Look Back

Briefly, you'll want to flip back to your last daily page to see if there are tasks that need carrying forward or items that need processing. You may have already taken care of this in a shutdown ritual (more on this later!) performed the day before, but a cursory glance is warranted.

Look Ahead

Review your master calendar to identify the blocks of time that have been committed to specific activities already. These might be meetings, appointments, fun activities (book club night?), or hard stops at the end of the day when you have to start driving your kids everywhere (fellow sports parents, I see you).

This process may be very straightforward, but in some cases you will need to dig a layer further to elucidate things that aren't necessarily specified in detail in your master calendar.

For example, if your master calendar doesn't contain work details (perhaps it only contains the hours that you work, which can be the case if the work details are confidential), you will need to review those work details first thing. On a clinical day, I need to look at two sources: my paper calendar weekly spread (my actual master calendar) and EPIC, our electronic health record. When I also had administrative responsibilities, I'd also have to pull up my work Outlook to review details of any work meetings. It's not that my master calendar is inaccurate; it contains my work hours along with any meetings on the schedule. It just cannot include the details, and those need to be scanned before the day can be planned strategically.

Second, you may be in an industry or life stage where calendar items appear overnight. If your master calendar is paper but your workplace has pop-up meetings that can bloom in any empty slot, you'll want to scan your work calendar first thing to see if there are fresh items in there. Side note: it depends on the workplace culture, but some people have great success in blocking off certain hours of the workday to protect focused work time and prevent meetings from filling every available crevice. This is a practice that for some can be a game changer in preventing these (typically unwelcome) morning surprises.

This may sound complicated, but you will quickly learn which sources need checking, and the whole overview should be very brief. Upon completing this step, you will quickly gain an understanding of what kind of day it is. Are there (gulp) twelve back-to-back meetings? Do you have a ton of open space? Did a big event get canceled, leaving you with a time windfall?

Create a Visual

Once I know I have a clear understanding of the day's scheduled events, I find it helpful to create some sort of visual aid to help me see the space and transition points available in each day. If you use a digital calendar, simply pulling up the full day view and taking a moment to digest the information may be enough. But I will put in a plug for drawing things out along a timeline, or printing out that digital page so you can sketch directly on it! I find that this is a simple but very powerful way to see how things fit and where any flexibility lies.

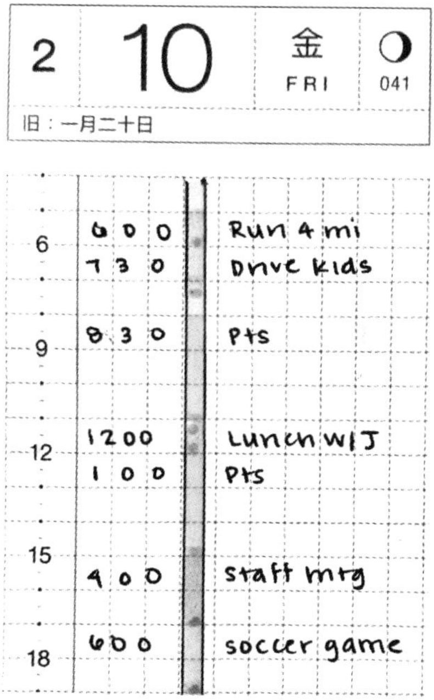

A timeline-style layout is available in a number of paper planners.

I personally love to draw out my day in the Hobonichi Cousin planner, an A5-size book with all twenty-four hours represented on the upper left side of the page, but the options are nearly limitless, and you could also use a blank notebook. If you'd like just a few places to start browsing, a few other daily planner options that show an hourly timeline are the Full Focus Planner, Simplified Planner, Passion Planner, and the Erin Condren Daily LifePlanner Duo (and there are many, many more!).

Look Within

Once you have a clear understanding of the level of structure already baked into the upcoming day, it's time to decide what else (if anything!) to add to your plate. Before you dive into your lists and potentially overload yourself with things that might fit into the day in the most optimistic version of your next twenty-four hours, take a minute to check in with yourself.

Are you fatigued? Are you feeling well in general? Is your headspace more "let's get after it!", or are you in more of a recovery phase? It's not imperative that everything you put on your daily list gets done. (To be fully transparent, I almost never get through every single item on my daily list! I'm perfectly content if ~70 percent of things get checked off, and some days I might do less than that—and that's okay!) That said, it just doesn't make sense to create an aggressive agenda on a day that you are feeling unwell or just entirely not up to it. Thinking through your physical and mental capabilities on a given day will help you make selections that are more reasonable and it will also help you prioritize—if you know you're only up for one thing, you'll be more apt to choose the one thing that is most crucial. You don't have to do anything formal in this step, but if it helps, you could write down a word at the top of your daily page that describes your current mood or readiness for action or even an adjective that describes the kind of day you'd like to have. ("Hygge"? "Action-packed"? So many possibilities!)

Look around and Create Your Daily List!

Next, it's time to review your weekly list and also acknowledge any unchecked boxes from the day prior, if you have any. You will be primed at this point, and all of the preparation you just did will likely make it fairly easy to decide what kinds of tasks belong on your daily list.

An important note: the tasks you choose for the day do NOT all have to come from your weekly list! In surveying the day's events, you might realize that you have to do careful edits on a long document due by the end of the workday, and you know this will take up almost all of your unstructured time. In that scenario, this task might be the only thing that makes the cut on that particular day.

But on some days, you may see that you have more blank space on your calendar than usual, and you might knock out three tasks from your weekly list in a highly efficient administrative block over lunch. The number and scope of tasks you choose need not be equal from day to day, and, in fact, it's best if you don't expect them to be! You want to choose to do items based on what is realistic and what you feel ready to do, and that is going to vary a lot from day to day.

Some might wonder whether this process places too much focus on the "urgent" matters of life (time-sensitive tasks, but not true priorities) at the expense of the important. First, let's acknowledge that there are decent number of tasks that fall into both categories. Second, trust the process (and yourself)! You spent plenty of time reflecting and thinking about your priorities when you created your goals at the very highest level (annual), and will be reviewing your goals at multiple time horizons on a regular basis. If you find that there are "important but not urgent" areas of your life that are being regularly bypassed to put out fires, you'll address that when you need to; we'll also be going into plenty of detail on tackling lingering and intimidating projects in the next chapter.

Note Habits and Routines

One final step I include in my daily planning process is to create some sort of space to track daily habits and routines. This practice serves as a gentle reminder for me about things that I hope to slot into random free moments throughout the day. As mentioned, my current core daily habits include meditation (ten minutes or less), going outside, reading, listening to music, and doing a language learning app. These are subject to change, of course, but right now, I like to create a little box at the top of my daily planning page that has a letter or symbol corresponding to each of these; I generally aim to check off each letter as the day goes on. Similar to my philosophy on task completion, I am not aiming for perfection here! I just know that having a reminder on my page means that sometimes I will choose to open my language-learning app instead of scroll, and that is helpful to me.

I will also note other routines along my timeline, such as exercise (usually an early strength session or workout) or when I hope to start the bedtime process with my youngest, since that has been a pain point in the past! I do not note every single routine action on my daily plan, but having a few key reminders is helpful. You can experiment to figure out which ones serve you—after all, you get 365 chances every year to help you find out what works!

Example Daily Habit Tracker

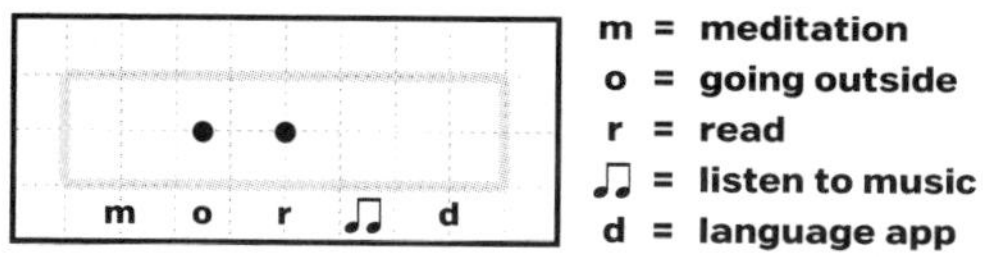

Ten Minutes of Planning

It may sound like a lot, but this process can be completed in about ten minutes! I know this because I've timed myself, starting with the moment I open my planner to the time I feel my daily scaffold is complete (including my daily timeline, task list, and a space to note habits and key routines). On some occasions, you might find a big surprise has landed on your schedule that derails the process, but this is hopefully not an everyday thing (and if it is...perhaps it isn't really that much of a surprise!).

You may feel like ten minutes seems too sizable, especially if it means a slightly earlier morning- wake-up time. But for a moment, let's revisit the proportions of this planning time: each day has 1,440 minutes. If eight hours of these are dedicated to sleep and therefore require little planning, that leaves you with 960 minutes.

Dedicating 10 of these 960 would mean spending just over 1 percent of your waking hours planning the other 99 percent. Surely even a tiny benefit in efficiency or clarity of mind on priorities would be worth this 1 percent investment! There is definitely an emotional benefit as well: you are actively choosing your path for the day rather than being pulled along based on calendar events that seemingly sneak up on you at regular intervals.

These ten minutes will also help shift your everyday balance of proactivity and reactivity. As mentioned, no one can be 100 percent proactive all the time—unexpected events and demands on your time will pop up sometimes no matter how well you plan! But perhaps every few weeks, your planning session will yield important information that helps the rest of the day go more smoothly; this might be as simple as remembering to order an ingredient online for that upcoming baking project or moving a meeting to ensure the right participants will be present. Added up, these little discoveries yield time dividends well over 1 percent.

Finally, remember the magic of the nested goals system, which means that on many days, some of the tasks on your lists can be traced all the way up to your highest priorities, the goals you set with a lot of thought and care at the beginning of the year. In this valuable 1 percent, your daily session is where the forward motion actually occurs, and it's a beautiful thing to see yourself progress in some of your highest priority areas, one day at a time.

Iterate and Adjust

I know what you're thinking. It all sounds well and good until you hear your child call from their room at 6:30 a.m. (a mere five minutes after you've finished planning your day, of course!) saying, "Mommy, I'm siiiiiiiick." And perhaps punctuating that statement with a hacking cough or worse.

This kind of situation happens, and it means an immediate rejuggling of priorities. It's true: once in a while, you will spend time creating a detailed plan and you won't get to carry it out. It's frustrating! I know this from experience, but I still believe daily planning is worth doing. Here are a few ways you can pivot and help yourself through a day that looks nothing like you planned.

- Once the immediate fire is put out (you've figured out who will take off from work; all bodily fluids are cleaned up), you can scan your plan and figure out if there is anything there that absolutely MUST HAPPEN NO MATTER WHAT. Having things already listed out is a lot easier than starting from scratch when you are in crisis mode.
- You can create a new simplified and shifted version of your day, with focus on your new priority (helping your sick child) but also figuring out when that one essential thing (if there is one) might fit into your adjusted day. Perhaps you can still do it during naptime, screen time, or by swapping with a partner. Or in jotting down a revised plan you'll realize that it's impossible, but at least you'll be able to give notice to anyone who was counting on you with a decent amount of warning. If you plan on paper, this plan B version of your day can be written out on a fresh sheet if you'd like—actually having a new document to refer to mentally helps me quite a bit!
- Your plan will help you pick up the pieces once things are closer

to normal! You'll be able to easily look back and see what you didn't do and migrate things forward. This will be a helpful resource once you're back to some sort of normal.

- It's important to see a necessary pivot like this as morally neutral. You didn't do anything wrong by having a plan that didn't work out, and you didn't "fail," either...and neither did the plan! It's just part of life that sometimes things change. For most, though, events occur as planned more times than not, and days with major priority pivots are exceptions. If you're becoming frustrated by days that didn't go as planned, it might be helpful to track "entirely off the rails" days and see how frequently they are actually occurring. If they are truly happening more often than not, you may be able to drill down to figure out why your general expectations of the day are not matching reality. It may not be something easily fixable (cold and flu season with babies and toddlers is ROUGH!), but you may then learn you might want to be less aggressive with your goals and plans for a stretch and leave more room for the inevitable pivot days.

Time-Block Planning

In discussing daily planning, the method of time-block planning deserves mention and consideration. Cal Newport described this technique in his 2016 book *Deep Work* and even created a paper planner to help time-block planning devotees follow the method.[6]

Similar to zero-based budgeting, the idea in time-block planning is to give every minute of your workday a job. Before the day begins, you review your goals and essentially create a schedule for the entire day in which you carry them out, with blocks that correspond to each of the day's tasks. You'll even slot in time for rest or breaks!

Time-Block Planning Example

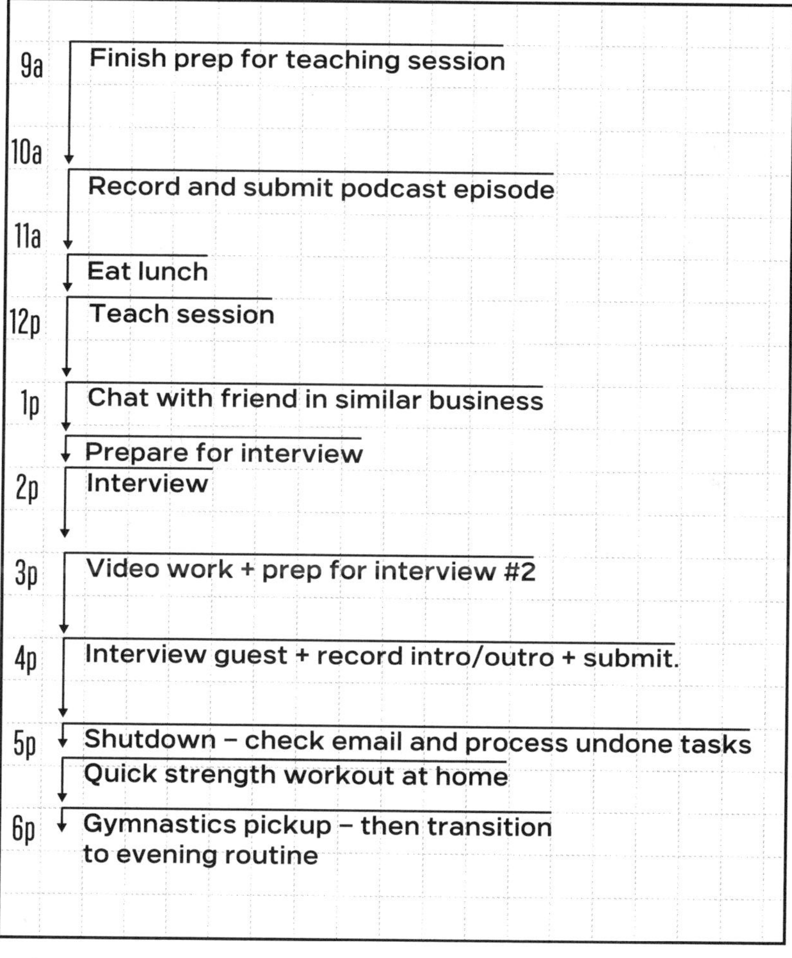

Newport finds this method to be a major boon to efficiency, and it does make sense that less time spent puttering around deciding what you'll do next can be helpful. In creating the plan, you're also priming your system to do the work you lay out. If you are the sort of person who can follow your plan consistently, you'll also be less likely to put off the tough tasks that may be higher priority—after all, if that hard thing is scheduled for 10:00 a.m., that's what you'll be doing at that time!

I think this method can be helpful for many, and I appreciate that Newport acknowledges that it's a pretty stressful way to go about working and therefore should not be applied to nonwork waking hours. He does not, for example, recommend time blocking your leisure time or time with family. However, there are some personality types that might find it incredibly tough to stick to a plan with such little wiggle room, even on a workday.

My own personal preference is to use this method *sometimes*. I find time-block planning particularly useful when I look at my schedule and tasks on a given day and feel a bit overwhelmed because there are multiple items with deadlines. Writing out a time-block plan helps give me confidence that I, in fact, can fit in the things that feel important and urgent that day, and I do find that it helps with efficiency! It's just a bit more stressful than I'd like my everyday workdays to be, and therefore I use it only when it feels necessary. On other days, I'll follow my schedule and slot in tasks when they feel right; I will have a basic idea of how this may play out when I create my timeline, but not every minute is accounted for. This feels like a helpful balance for me. I encourage everyone to give time-block planning a try, particularly on a day that feels intimidating and full at the outset.

Transitions and Closing the Day

Do you ever notice how certain things take longer than you expect them to, and you can't even identify exactly what it is you're doing while time is ticking by? Often, we discount time spent in transition.

There are the obvious transitions, like time spent on a commute. But there are also sneaky little transitions, like minutes spent bundling up a small child to go out into the cold (sometimes not so little, depending on the mood of the toddler!). It can be helpful to start noticing how long these things tend to take so you can (yes) plan accordingly! It simply isn't possible to line up eight activities that take exactly sixty minutes each and then expect them to fit neatly into an eight-hour workday; there will be inevitable bathroom breaks and tech hiccups and meetings that run over.

It's also helpful to leave some time for processing! There's informal processing, such as the time it takes to think through an offer you've received, or triage an ever-expanding email inbox. (Side note: if you let it, this kind of processing can eat up significant chunks of your day; more on controlling digital inputs to avoid this in chapter 8.)

There's also, for many of us, a need for some kind of closing ritual toward the end of the day. This practice helps us take stock of what has been accomplished and accept that some of the things that were on the day's list will have to be migrated elsewhere (to tomorrow, another time frame's list, or perhaps eliminated altogether).

Similar to the ten minutes that won't magically appear at the beginning of the day without some thought and planning, many people will benefit from purposefully slotting in a quick closing ritual. This has been called many things: David Allen refers to it as "processing time,"[7] while Cal Newport names it his "Shutdown Ritual."[8] Whatever you call it, creating some sort of official closing ritual for your day can be both logistically helpful and emotionally calming. You're carefully managing the day's notes and tasks to ensure nothing gets missed but also giving yourself official permission to move from the productive portion of your day toward evening, which is typically more of a wind-down period. While there are some who prefer to include a shorter "second shift" in the evenings (focusing on work obligations or household tasks), it can still be valuable to have loose ends tied up so that the only thing left to do is to execute.

In this chapter, we've drilled down to the smallest time horizon in our framework and the one that fully closes the gap between planning and doing. Your planning sessions for each day may be short, but they are a powerful tool to help you stay true to your priorities and remain present, so you can live with more peace and make the most of your time.

Daily Planning Checklist

Four Essentials Needed to Plan Your Day:

1. Accurate and well-maintained master calendar
2. Weekly task list
3. Understanding of desired routines and habits
4. A defined time slot (around ten minutes) to complete this planning session

Daily Planning Steps:

☐ **Look back** to ensure tasks and notes from the day prior have been processed. Make sure incomplete tasks are still represented in some way (on your weekly list) or choose to eliminate them.

(Note: this step may not be necessary if you conduct a thorough closing ritual.)

☐ **Look ahead.** Review your master calendar to see what is already planned for the day (meetings, appointments, anything with a hard start or stop time). Check for sneaky last-minute add-ons; if these tend to occur with any regularity, you likely know where to look for them.

☐ **Create (or view) a visual.** Create a timeline for the day in your favorite planner or notebook or view one on your electronic calendar app of choice. Note where there are empty spaces (unstructured/unclaimed time), and don't forget about transitions!

- ☐ **Look within.** Take a moment to assess how you feel. Exhausted? Energetic? No need to do anything formal with this information (unless you want to!) but you will keep it in mind as you choose tasks for the day.
- ☐ **Look around and create your daily list!** It's time to integrate all of the information you just took in and commit! Choose tasks that fit the day's time constraints and your energy, and address any urgent needs. You will likely have a mix of tasks from your weekly list and one-off matters that pertain to the day at hand. Don't worry about hitting a specific number—some days, you might have just one thing on your list and on days with more unstructured time you'll have more.
- ☐ **Remember your habits and routines.** Make space (either in your head or on your daily planning page) to note any habits you'd like to fit in throughout the day. This helps especially with "unscheduled" habits that you hope to fit into free pockets of time, like texting a family member or completing a brief language learning lesson.

Additional Daily Planning Considerations

- **Remember transitions!** Don't discount the time spent in both formal and informal transitions, from your commute to those moments spent waiting for your coffee order or putting on a child's winter gear.

- **Consider a closing ritual.** Many people will benefit from a few minutes at the end of the day dedicated to processing loose ends, including uncompleted tasks and any notes written to yourself throughout the day.

- **Try time-block planning** if you have a packed day. This method assigns every minute of the working day a task or specific rest period and cuts down on dithering or time spent deciding what to do next; it can also help you tackle challenging tasks earlier in the day, as long as you are committed to following your own plan.

- **Remember that iterations and adjustments are normal;** it's simply a part of life that some days will not go according to plan (even if you did an amazing job putting that plan together!). Be compassionate with yourself and remember that you will still likely be able to put your prior planning to good use in the future once things calm down; take some time to create a plan B acknowledging the day's new reality if a significant pivot is necessary.

When You Find Yourself Stuck

Burnout, Overload, Big Project Intimidation, and Procrastination

This chapter was inspired by a listener who wrote into *Best Laid Plans* podcast, and I am grateful she took the time and effort to share her story. In response to a podcast episode where I myself noted that I was struggling with some of my own big goals, she wrote:

"You mentioned 'feeling stuck.' I recently struggled with this feeling. I would make my daily plan and then feel so overwhelmed that I was almost paralyzed and couldn't get myself to actually start the things on the list. I realized I needed to break down my overwhelming task list into smaller projects so it wouldn't seem so daunting, but then I became overwhelmed by the sheer number of tasks. I kept rewriting my lists thinking I needed to break things down differently, but nothing was working to help me get the things done. I listened to some podcast episodes from various planning experts. I thought maybe I just needed a better planner or colorful highlighters to help."

She continued: "At the same time, I already had a therapist appointment scheduled for an unrelated issue. It turns out that the therapist diagnosed me with burnout. My feelings of being 'stuck' and 'paralyzed' were most likely a response to all of the recent stress in my life."

While I do love a fresh pack of colorful highlighters, I was struck by this listener's comment, which she thoughtfully sent me during Mental Health Awareness Month (May). As she eloquently put it, "Sometimes all the planners and pens and tips aren't enough."

Feeling stuck is common, and there are so many reasons you may find yourself feeling this way. You could be in a difficult season, or maybe, like my listener, you are facing burnout or another mental-health issue. Other potential challenges include overload, big projects that feel stressful and intimidating, or perhaps you're facing a common nemesis: procrastination. In this chapter, we will discuss how planning interfaces with all of these obstacles, and where you might turn for help.

Burnout and Mental Health

I think there has been progress made with respect to mental-health awareness and self-compassion in the productivity world in recent years. Hustle culture, girl boss aesthetic, and the expectation of 24-7 accessibility all seem rather dated at this point, and I personally think this is a positive shift. In *The PLAN*, Kendra Adachi does a wonderful job of describing how hormones and mood impact one's productivity, and she encourages her followers to embrace these ebbs and flows of energy rather than fight them.[1] Oliver Burkeman's *Meditations for Mortals* is all about finitude and seeing our limitations as a feature rather than a flaw. Even Cal Newport—mentioned in the previous chapter for his sometimes stressful (he has admitted this himself!) time-block planning method—recently published a thoughtful treatise on working on fewer projects in *Slow Productivity*. In this book, he effectively demonstrates that taking on too many things causes a degradation in both quality and the worker's experience, and therefore no one wins when there is a culture of overload.[2]

All of these principles can be distilled into one bittersweet fact: we can do a lot over the span of our human lives, but we cannot do everything. Planning itself is about bringing more thoughtfulness and intention to the way we choose to spend our time, and in many cases this can be helpful! But there are times when forward motion toward bigger goals just isn't accessible. Sometimes we need rest, assistance, physical or emotional support, or time to recover or grieve. This is normal and expected and should never be viewed as a failure. It is simply part of being human.

So, from a practical standpoint, how do you know when you need a break from your typical productive habits, and what can you do to embrace rest when it is needed? The ideas below are suggestions of ways to use or adjust planning techniques during challenging times.

Designate a Time Period to Wallow

This approach can be helpful with short-term stress or moderately challenging circumstances. I define wallowing as "letting yourself lean into the suck," and personally I will sometimes find immense benefit in taking some time to just do very little and let myself sulk over a twenty-four-to-forty-eight-hour period, with the intent to turn things around at the end. When wallowing, you can listen to sad music (vintage Aimee Mann always does it for me), journal, eat chocolate (duh), binge a Netflix series (maybe one about cults?), or do whatever you feel like doing (or not doing). Your plan for the day might just say "wallow" as you take things hour by hour.

I have wallowed when I have faced unexpected setbacks, such as when I have found my own carefully laid plans derailed by a forecasted hurricane that never ended up actually materializing. It may not be the wallow itself that helps so much as the declaration to move on once it's over, but I still find the approach therapeutic at times. That said, wallowing will not be sufficient in dealing with long-term disappointment or truly devastating events such as the loss of a loved one.

Make a Declaration Within Your Planning Tools

When the COVID-19 pandemic caused widespread shutdowns, I started making bold marks in my planner. "Canceled!" was scrawled jubilantly over an entire week in March. When things started to feel less temporary, I switched planners and it helped me cope with the new uncertainty; this tangible swap was an acknowledgment and acceptance that life would not be proceeding according to my previous plans for quite some time, and it was beneficial to avoid regularly confronting all sorts of calendar items that had been rendered meaningless.

All this to say: changing planners or writing "NEVER MIND!" in big bold letters over something that will no longer come to fruition is not sufficient action to get you through very hard times, but it could be one small piece of the puzzle.

Connect with a Loved One

When you are incredibly stressed out or sad, it can be so hard and downright undesirable to seek the company of others—and yet whenever I make plans under those circumstances, I am always incredibly glad I did. If getting dressed to look presentable feels like too much, you can connect through audio; my favorite way to connect in this way is by taking a walk with my phone in hand.

This can also be a safety mechanism. If you are really struggling, it's likely that your loved one will pick up on that and help escalate the level of care that is needed. For those who struggle with mood issues frequently, some kind of weekly connection ritual could be incredibly helpful as an automatic check-in as well as a potential mood lifter.

Find Inspiration in the Journeys of Others

When you're in a real-life slump, it can be helpful to read books or articles about others who have gone through similar challenges and emerged on the other side. Once again, this strategy probably will not be enough to pull you from the depths of a true depressive state, but this can be considered one adjunct balm. One of my favorite works in this genre is *Wintering: The Power of Rest and Retreat in Difficult Times* by Katherine May, about a woman who takes an extended break during the winter for primarily mental health reasons. I read it while going through a low period with some work stressors and found it quite comforting to follow the author's journey.

Set a Date to Reassess

If you're struggling with low moods or a difficult circumstance that seems endless or ill-defined, it can be helpful to set a future date to reassess. This can then be noted directly in your calendar or planner. Sometimes just having a future point identified as the point of escalation will stop you from stressfully spiraling about when to take more drastic action: Is it now? Or now? Or NOW?!

I used to suffer from very low moods leading up to my period; I met clinical criteria for premenstrual dysphoric disorder (PMDD). Things would be dandy from approximately day two of my cycle until day fourteen or so, and the rest of the month had a dark cloud hanging over it. (Why yes, this pattern meant I was struggling more than half the time!) I remember one day deciding I would track my moods for a month and seek help if, in fact, I did find myself in a funk for the length of time I suspected, and this deadline approach was the push I needed to finally see my OBGYN and ask for assistance (which brings us to the last and possibly most important item on this list). Without quantifying my struggles and drawing a line in the sand, I might have let many more difficult months pass without action.

Seek Expert Assistance

When you find yourself unmotivated to participate actively in your life for any significant stretch, it is important to reach out for help from an expert. As our podcast listener noted at the beginning of this chapter, an inability to carry out your plans or a listless "stuck" feeling can be a sign of depression, burnout, or both. Not once have I regretted consulting a mental-health professional, and there have been multiple times

I wished that I had taken this step sooner. Sometimes the inability to plan or move forward in life has nothing to do with organization or systems and everything to do with mental health, and thankfully there are resources out there (therapists, medications, and other forms of support) that can help.

Overload

A few years ago, I made the difficult decision to leave a leadership role at work. This director-level role running the hospital's residency program in pediatrics was an honor to attain and came with great responsibility that I took very seriously. It came with ample protected time (as in, dedicated work hours away from patient care) and a small financial benefit. Our program was quite new, so it was exciting to be building something fresh and innovative, and I loved working with the residents and watching them grow! But approximately three years in, I decided I had to give it up. There were multiple underlying reasons for this: It was a stressful position made even more stressful through the pandemic, and it was a role that really required 24-7 availability that I did not feel I could provide.

But the primary reason I left the role was sheer lack of time and bandwidth; I had reached a level of overload that was incongruent with the way I wanted to live. This didn't occur overnight! In 2020, I started *Best Laid Plans*, my own solo podcast about "all things planning and planning-adjacent," thinking it would be a fun side project and distraction from pandemic life. I had some extra time; in fact, we were actually "furloughed" at work and required to take off every other Friday. I also worked part-time (80 to 90 percent full time equivalent). Things were doable under those circumstances.

Then, things shifted. Life didn't exactly return to normal right away, but in-person events started to crop up, and I started commuting regularly again. My kids returned to school and a few of their activities, necessitating daily driving that had been markedly reduced for months. And even though I thought it might be a limited one-off niche project, it turns out that people seemed to really enjoy *Best Laid Plans*, and I enjoyed creating the episodes and thinking of all sorts of planning-related topics! I spent time refining my thoughts on planning and thought perhaps I'd turn my systems into a book one day (spoiler: you're reading it).

I planned, time blocked, and worked on my efficiency, but ultimately I had to confront the truth: I did not have time for my podcasting and creative work on top of the challenges of a (difficult!) full-time job working in medicine and leading a residency program. This was pure overload, and no amount of strategy or organization was going to fix my problem. I left the leadership role in 2022 and currently see patients three days most weeks as a part-time provider. On the other two days, I write, podcast, teach courses, and handle various kid-related issues, like appointments that can only be scheduled on weekdays.

How do you know when you've hit overload? Honestly, it's tough! But I think with regular reflection, at some point you will just know. I do think it can be a dangerous path to assume that one bad day means your life is all wrong; there is a trope where working parents will describe leaving a lucrative corporate career path after feeling regret upon missing one championship soccer game or preschool holiday show. These stories may sound poignant, but everyone has conflicts in priorities once in a while, and sometimes there is an intermediate option beyond a drastic career pivot.

Instead, it's best to watch for patterns. Are you regularly unable to meet your sleep needs? Are you missing multiple deadlines because you just can't find enough hours to get your work done? Do you have a nagging sense that you truly aren't able to give one of your life roles or big projects the attention you feel it deserves?

Those things all suggest that there is overload and that something (or multiple things!) must go. It can be helpful in these circumstances to bring in an outside voice, perhaps that of a trusted friend or mentor. You can lay out your current roles, projects, and priorities—and see whether things look sustainable to an outsider. One exercise is to try viewing each of your major activities with fresh eyes: if you were designing your life from scratch, would you include it? This thought experiment will help you avoid succumbing to the sunk cost fallacy: just because you paid a price (in sweat equity or actual currency) for some opportunity in life doesn't mean you have to take it or hold on to it forever. Revisiting your Ideal Week (see chapter 3) can be valuable here as well.

It feels appropriate to bring up the concept of finitude once more. It isn't always stated outright, but a major part of planning is deciding what *not* to do, because the truth is that we only have one limited timespan to spend on earth. Coming to terms with your own limitations and addressing overload when it happens is one way to ensure we have time and energy left for the things we care about the most.

Big Projects + Intimidation

One day, it occurred to me that I was spinning my wheels on several big projects at once, and they all had several things in common.

They were intimidating.

They were ill-defined and had no natural deadline.

They were emotionally fraught.

I was not reporting back to anyone but myself (and perhaps my husband).

The hairiest of these projects was to get our estate planning completed. Confession: we started the process. But more than six (SIX!) years after we paid our initial legal fees and provided some introductory information, we had not finished.

For our three kids (well, two when we started!), it was important to my husband and me that we take all of the necessary steps to make sure they are provided for in a thoughtful way if disaster should strike. Everyone in my life told us this was an important thing to do. It wasn't physically painful or as complex as a rocket launch. But WHY couldn't we do it!?

One day, feeling frustrated, I shared a blog post about several larger goals I was feeling stuck on, with estate planning at the top of the list. I recognized the features of the goals I had just listed: intimidating, ill-defined without a natural deadline, emotionally fraught, and without outside accountability. I am thrilled to share that a mere seven months after I completed this analysis, I conquered most of the goals from that post. (Decluttering my home remains a work in progress, but my kids are a force of entropy to be reckoned with, so I decided to table this goal until they are older!)

What helped? Attacking each of those sticky features previously mentioned at the root! Here is how this worked, using the example of estate planning:

Intimidating. Yes, completing the estate-planning process was intimidating. It seemed like something I should understand on my own as an adult, yet I really didn't. So, to address this, I decided I would let an expert guide me along the way, and I also decided to let go of any ideas about completing the process perfectly or impressing anyone along the way. After all, estate planning involves creating documents that communicate your wishes in a legally binding fashion, but documents can be revised! I requested a meeting with our attorney where she would explain everything in layman's terms and clearly lay out our next steps in the process.

Ill-defined and without a natural deadline. Without a clear end in mind, it's very hard to work toward a goal. My husband and I had to decide exactly what we were hoping to get out of the process (documents drawn up and signed officially to clarify our end-of-life desires around finances and our children), and we needed some sort of hard landscape feature. It hadn't worked to simply put this project on my annual list; I just moved it from year to year. But what did work was to set up a signing date with the law office and take time off work to get it completed. I knew that once we had this deadline on the calendar, we would be sure to work through any necessary steps and talk through any decisions in time. And we did!

Emotionally fraught. Okay, there really isn't an easy way to make talking about your own demise easy and fun. But we acknowledged the emotionally challenging nature of the task at hand, and that in itself was helpful. Our attorney was patient and sensitive, and thus she also served as a supportive outsider to help guide us through talking about difficult topics.

Lack of outside accountability. Once again, bringing in our legal helpers and putting actual dates on the calendar (not just a vague promise to get back to them with information when we felt ready) was key here. We didn't want to disappoint our attorney and her team or waste her time, so we were motivated to complete our tasks and commit to decisions far more efficiently than we were able to on our own.

Procrastination

Oh, this section could probably be an entire book, and in fact there are many books dedicated to this topic alone; my favorite title is probably *Procrastination: Why You Do It, What to Do About It NOW* by Jane B. Burka and Lenora M. Yuen. Joking aside, procrastination is a common issue and a great source of stress for many people. It is particularly common in those who struggle with executive function, including those with ADHD, but many people without these differences struggle with it too, at least to some extent.

Within reason, some degree of putting things off may actually be quite adaptive. If you have a well-honed sense of how long things take, then leaving certain things until "just when you need them" can actually be beneficial in some cases. Think about studying: you won't necessarily retain tiny details if you completed your last flash card session three weeks ago; you're better off doing it the morning of your test. This is to say that assigning a higher moral value to things done well in advance versus in a "just-in-time" fashion, in my opinion, is a mistake.

On the flip side, it is definitely possible to cut things too close and to suffer undue stress with reduced quality output because of procrastination. When procrastination occurs across all areas of life in a chronic way that causes suffering, it's likely something that should be addressed by an expert such as a therapist, mental-health provider, or executive skills coach. However, if you're finding yourself procrastinating only under certain circumstances, the following questions may be helpful to consider:

1. **Is this a perfectionism issue?** Sometimes, procrastination arises from the idea that things have to be perfect. Women are more likely to struggle with perfectionism,[3] though it's relatively common in both genders. It can be paralyzing to feel like you need to complete a task perfectly each time, and can lead to perfectionists putting off tasks until some sort of exceptional readiness level is reached, which might never actually occur. If this rings true with you, ask yourself what would happen if your first attempt at completing the tasks didn't go exactly right. Is there a "first draft" version you could start with to get the ball rolling? Many authors swear by the concept of a very rough initial draft, since getting something onto the page is better than staring at a blank screen hoping for the perfect sentence to take shape. Instead, the idea is to dive boldly into writing something that may be messy; the author can always improve upon it later!

2. **What are you afraid of?** Fear can go hand-in-hand with perfectionism but can also stand alone. I think some part of me may have feared finishing the estate-planning process because I was worried my husband and I wouldn't agree on various high-stakes things, plus I was simply scared to think about worst-case scenarios because it sounded stressful. Bringing your fears to light can help you get past them or seek out support where it is needed.

3. **Do you understand the first step?** Sometimes an item will linger untouched on an annual or seasonal list longer than is necessary because it's just not entirely clear how to begin. Instead of taking the time to think through it, you might brush past it and move on to something that sounds simpler. If this turns out to be the case, I recommend coming up with the very first tiniest little step (often it's doing some cursory research or making an initial contact) and writing it next to the big overlooked goal on your list. When the initial step seems so doable, you'll be less inclined to avoid it the next time around.

4. **Is the timeline realistic?** I do want to organize my home, but I did not choose a realistic timeline to get this job done, taking into account the ages of my children and all of the other things going on in my life. After kicking this project forward a number of times, I recognized that I have to choose a new timeline.

5. **Do you really want to do it?** This may seem obvious, but if you're kicking the can forward on a larger-scale project year after year, it's important to be honest with yourself about whether it truly belongs

on the list. Maybe it's a dream you used to have but don't anymore, or a reflection of goals set for you by your parents as a younger child. You can always let it sit in your someday possibilities list if you want to be reminded of it in the future.

Checklist for When You Feel Stuck

Burnout and Mental Health

- ☐ Let yourself wallow for a designated period of time.
- ☐ Use your planning tools to create a declaration or manifesto.
- ☐ Plan for some connection time, even if it isn't your first inclination.
- ☐ Find inspiration in the journeys of others.
- ☐ Set a date to reassess.
- ☐ Seek expert help—the most important item on this list and essential when things feel really difficult.

Overload

- ☐ Watch for patterns (chronic fatigue or sleep deprivation, multiple missed deadlines, or a persistent feeling that you're not giving various areas of your life the attention they deserve).
- ☐ Bring in a trusted outside voice, such as a close friend or mentor.
- ☐ Pretend you are designing your life from scratch; try to avoid the sunk cost fallacy when it comes to your projects and activities.
- ☐ Draw out an ideal week to determine whether things truly fit.

Big Intimidating Projects

- ☐ Address the intimidation factor head on. Does the project feel too big? Too high stakes? Figuring out what makes it scary is the first step toward addressing these challenges.
- ☐ Define what "done" looks like to you, identify the first step, and clarify your timeline.

- ☐ Identify what feels emotionally challenging about the project, bring feelings to light, and obtain support if needed.
- ☐ Create accountability, preferably with a hard deadline on the calendar involving others if possible!

Procrastination

- ☐ Assess for perfectionism--is it hindering your progress or ability to get started? Consider a very rough low pressure first draft.
- ☐ Identify any fears around completing the project, whether they relate to steps along the way, the final product, or changes that might occur as a result of your goal being met.
- ☐ Clarify the first step of your big project and include it next to the goal on your list.
- ☐ Evaluate the timeline: is it realistic, or are you avoiding the project because you know the proposed timeline is unrealistic?
- ☐ If there's a project you're perpetually pushing forward, be honest yourself about whether you really want to do it!

8 Challenges

From Planning Privilege to
Time Sucks and Beyond

In the last chapter, we discussed all kinds of challenges that pop up in life with ideas for planning strategies that might help. This chapter is also focused on challenges, but this next set of issues includes those that often arise within the planning process itself! From struggling to get started to dealing with distractions or even planning naysayers, we'll tackle many of the roadblocks and struggles you might face on your planning journey.

Challenge #1: Learning Curve

"I just can't handle those kinds of details."
"My mind just doesn't work like that."
"I've tried planners but end up abandoning them; they just don't work for me!"
"The Planning Industrial Complex is trying to sell us a lie!"

It's true. Planning does not come naturally to many people. Neither do many things! I personally struggle with anything that involves visuospatial processing, like navigation and manipulating images in space. These deficits were made abundantly clear when I took on the challenge of learning organic chemistry, a prerequisite for medical school. Nothing about it was natural, but with tutoring, the use of models, and a lot of practice, I became proficient enough to earn a reasonable grade in the course.

The same holds true with skills related to goal setting, planning, and task management—there's a learning curve, but skills and practices can be attained over time. However, often the lessons in this realm must be intentionally sought out. Observing my own school-age children, I have been surprised to see how little attention is given to these topics as part of their official school curriculum. There is an element of learning by doing, but not every elementary school kid has the inclination to optimize their own planning and organizing practices, despite the fact that it would make sense to build some functional habits before the work becomes more challenging in later grades.

On the flip side, I have noticed how teaching and modeling even small planning rituals can help kids prioritize and manage their obligations. One of my kids creates daily checklists when feeling overwhelmed; another prefers to keep track of things on a whiteboard. With exposure to various techniques and some time for iteration, each person can figure out what works for them. As with any learning process, there will be an element of trial and error involved.

It's not too late for adults, either! Lisa Woodruff, the founder of Organize 365, states it often and even made it the title of one of her books: "Organization is a learnable skill."[1] I believe the same holds true with planning and other forms of executive function. Participants in Best Laid Plans Academy, a seven-week course based on the principles found in this book, have written to me months after course completion letting me know how much the practices of regular goal setting and strategic task management have helped them live differently, with less stress and often tackling big projects that previously remained elusive.

These practices are helpful even for those who struggle with various elements of executive function, such as those with ADHD. Multiple members of my household carry this official diagnosis, and thus I have some very personal experience in seeing how ADHD can make many aspects of planning and organizing more challenging. I am not going to suggest that no one in our home procrastinates or forgets anything—that would be a bold-faced lie! But I do believe things are better than they would be otherwise because of some of the rituals we have built together as a family, and the fact that we regularly talk about effective planning methods and strategies. If you do struggle with ADHD, the management is certainly beyond the scope of this book, but there are some great resources that focus specifically on executive function in this context.[2]

For those not managing a specific diagnosis, one idea is to work on your techniques and methods with some built-in support. This could take the form of a partner who plans alongside you each weekend, or a formal coach who walks you through your monthly goal-setting practice. Retreats in a group or with a partner at the yearly or seasonal level can be incredibly helpful for those who know they will struggle to carve out the necessary time and focus on their own. You could also seek out some virtual accountability by sharing your lists and intentions with a friend in a chat or a shared document.

If you're worried that you just don't have what it takes to build an airtight task management system and set goals strategically at each time horizon, I encourage you to try anyway! Getting your planning and life-management systems up and running is a learning journey just like taking guitar lessons or mastering a new language. It may take time, but with practice things will almost always improve and ultimately impact so many other areas of your life.

Challenge #2: Planning Privilege

> *"My partner just doesn't see the point of all this planning. He just wants to be able to play things by ear."*—Planner
>
> *"All this planning takes away the fun—what happened to serendipity?"*—Naysayer
>
> *"Why do I feel like all of the work I do to keep everyone happy and comfortable is invisible labor?"*—Planner
>
> *"I just want to relax on the weekends and not feel stressed out about the week ahead. These details aren't important; I'm sure everything will turn out fine."*—Naysayer

In my years of teaching the skills of planning and helping others refine their systems, some patterns have emerged. One relatively common scenario is that one member of the household does most or all of the planning for the family unit, and the other devalues it, fights it, or may be disdainful of the process. The gender dynamics are usually (though certainly not always!) that the planner of the family is female, and the naysayer is male. I will refer to these two parties as the Planner and the Naysayer going forward.

I coined the term "planning privilege" to describe this phenomenon, because I think at the root of this issue many Naysayers enjoy all of the benefits of the planning process but do not want to acknowledge or participate in the labor or carry the associated mental load. This is a privileged position that places undue burden on the Planner without credit or reciprocity. Thus: planning privilege.

From the Planner's perspective, planning and arranging various aspects of family life can feel frustrating on multiple levels. Working toward longer-term plans that involve other household members is difficult if not impossible when the Naysayer won't engage in conversation around these shared experiences. It's hard to communicate about the week, month, or season up ahead when no one is interested in listening. Finally, there's the reality of planning fatigue, which rears its head more often when the act of planning feels thankless or futile.

To be clear, this is not typically a malicious dynamic, and the Naysayer may not even realize anything is wrong! When the essential elements of life are almost always figured out for you, it is easy to avoid planning and devalue its worth—after all, you aren't doing it, and things *are* working out just fine! There also may be a subconscious tendency to avoid acknowledging the reality of an unequally shared load, particularly when there are children involved. Writing out and discussing a plan might make it clear that the Planner is doing much of the household labor and child management while the Naysayer is experiencing "serendipitous" relaxation.

This dynamic may exist for years within households, and perhaps both parties are able to find a way to make peace with these widely different approaches. But for others, it remains a constant source of tension that has deeper implications beyond who is in charge of figuring out dinner. First, if there are kids involved—especially young ones—the only way for adults to carve out time to pursue their own activities is to plan (or to have your partner plan or provide a default caregiver role at all times). From a pure logistics standpoint, the Planner needs some kind of childcare coverage (which must almost always be planned in advance) to do things as simple as take an exercise class or to meet up with friends or loved ones. This imbalance can be incredibly draining on the Planner, and may even bring on burnout and mental-health struggles.

Second, pursuing our goals and dreams is deeply satisfying to most humans, whether the goals are minor (throw a neighborhood potluck) or weightier (work toward a new certification or degree). Many such endeavors require buy-in or help from loved ones, or at the very least, support makes pursuing goals easier and more fun. If the Naysayer never wants to engage in this kind of shared dreaming, it can feel very limiting for a partner looking for ways to make the most of his or her life.

Luckily, I am not speaking from personal experience on this topic in my own relationship. Over nearly twenty years of marriage as of this book's release (and possibly aided by the fact that my goal-setting and household management activities are discussed outright, because they are now part of my professional identity!), my husband has definitely acquired an appreciation for the effort required, and he is an active participant himself. I daresay he even enjoys planning with me, from seasonal sessions to travel planning to our regular Sunday night family discussions about the upcoming week.

In planning and dreaming together, we try to enjoy the process of setting goals and pursuing adventures. Last year we supported each other in working toward Boston-qualifying marathon times; this was quite a long-term project, but we both did it (at the same race, too—it was a great day)! Tackling this challenge together was gratifying, and supporting each other to reach our goals brought us closer together.

If you do have a partner who tends to be a Naysayer, see if you can (calmly) share the reasons behind your efforts to plan and organize for the family. It may be worth detailing your processes and explaining exactly how they benefit everyone, sharing the ways your work helps to make others' lives more convenient and comfortable. In some cases, it may be worth bringing in a professional; long term, a relationship cannot remain healthy if one person's desire for personal spontaneity and freedom stands consistently in the way of another's innate desire to work toward various wishes and dreams.

Challenge #3: Uncertainty

> *"It just feels so hard to plan when I'm not sure what the next year will look like—I'm job-hunting and may be moving to a whole new city! I have no idea what next month will look like, let alone next year."*

"I'm in the throes of trying to conceive, and there is so much uncertainty. Will we succeed? Will I be lucky enough to be planning around a future pregnancy and baby soon, or not? I want to think about my future, but I just feel stuck without a road map of what is up ahead."

I've heard so many variations of this question, and many of them make me well up, as I wish I could reach through my laptop and send a hug through the interwebs. Uncertainty is a very real challenge, and many uncertain scenarios are just so hard.

Really, nothing is certain for any of us, but many life situations highlight this difficult truth more than others. From a practical standpoint, I have found that it can help to focus on shorter-term planning and let yourself dream about things that do feel within your control.

You may not be able to clearly visualize life six months from now, but you can probably still picture the next day, week, and even month. You can focus your energy on these shorter time horizons, and let the longer-term horizons stay fuzzier until they naturally come into focus. Or, you can stick to planning the areas that do feel within your control—in pandemic times, most people weren't planning elaborate vacations, but they compensated by planning virtual events or coming up with ideas for local outdoor fun.

You can also create contingency goals or dreams; I did this during my own infertility journey. It took me over two frustrating years to get pregnant with my first child, and at one point, fed up with the uncertainty of it all and very much needing something positive to look forward to, my husband and I decided to book a (refundable) trip to

Hawaii. We reserved the hotel and told ourselves that we would take the trip if I wasn't pregnant by a certain time.

We didn't end up taking that trip, which was the best outcome I could have imagined! But having it booked as a contingency plan really helped my outlook during a really tough time. Just ensure that anything you plan in these kinds of circumstances can be canceled without too much penalty.

Challenge #4: Planning Perfectionism

> *"I just never feel like I get my setup to a place that feels exactly right."*
>
> *"I am afraid to mess up my brand-new notebooks and planners! My handwriting is messy, and I always make mistakes, and then I find myself not wanting to look at the pages."*
>
> *"Goals scare me—failure and uncertainty stress me out, so I never want to set goals I'm not entirely sure I can accomplish."*

Perfectionism as a barrier to achievement was discussed in the last chapter, but this concept is a little bit different: some people end up stuck because they are afraid of imperfection within their own systems. A desire to be perfect can prevent effective planning in a number of ways. One common example is that some people feel like they cannot get started with any sort of planning routine until the absolutely ideal setup has been created, and even then they may be fearful of using their (carefully curated!) tools because they will mar pristine pages or just generally do things wrong.

Tools are for using, planning practices must be flexible, and notebooks are for writing in—mistakes and all! I personally don't use correction tape, pencils, or erasable pens. Instead, when I make a mistake or something gets canceled, I just cross things out neatly with a single line and move on. If you aren't able to process your inbox in its entirety one week, there is no massive disaster and no personal failure. None of the techniques presented in this book require exact adherence to specifications to be helpful. You will get much more out of imperfect planning than you would if you avoided it altogether.

A second way perfectionism can be detrimental is that for some people, the mere idea of writing things down that they might not accomplish evokes a lot of anxiety and other negative feelings. It may be that a simple reframe would help here—you could list your goals, but perhaps create a category with a name like "hoping to do, but not certain." Your goals list is not a life report card, remember! In a given year or season, listing ten big goals and achieving eight of them is likely a smashing success. If you are excited about achieving or pursuing something, it is much more likely to happen if it's actually on your list and you think about it multiple times throughout the year. See if you can work on any rigid or fearful feelings around checking off 100 percent of the boxes in any list. If it helps, I almost never do, but getting most of the way there typically means getting plenty accomplished.

Challenge #5: Time Sucks

"I sometimes get up in the morning intending to plan out my day, but then I get distracted by notifications on my phone, and

before I know it I'm forty minutes into TikTok and it's too late to do anything but scramble out the door to work."

"I try to plan in enjoyable evening activities but often get sucked into family drama in a group text instead; after thirty minutes of furious back-and-forth, I'm so stressed that I need to scroll Reddit to escape."

"I create a realistic list of priority items for the day, but I end up lost in my email and by the time I come up for air I find it hard to focus and end up squeezed for time."

It may seem outside the scope of this book about planning, but I believe it has to be said: for many, digital distractions get in the way of effective planning. Furthermore, the chaotic stream of inputs on our ubiquitous devices is one of the main barriers to productivity and moving forward with one's desired plans, even ones that serve a broader life vision. I don't think anyone writes "spend three hours scrolling social media" in their planner, and yet it's exactly what many of us do, whether it's in one chunk or spread throughout the day. We consume content as it pops up, moving from notification to link to story based on the whims of the tech algorithms, not our own desires or interests. And it doesn't even take an audible ping or vibration for many of us to interrupt ourselves with the desire to "check" for new inputs (email, text messages, app notifications, social media updates—you name it!).

You can have the best task management system and the most organized and comprehensive planning practices in place, but it's unlikely that you will progress toward your goals in a meaningful way if you are constantly distracted and your attention is fragmented for hours each day. Therefore, as you are thinking about setting up your system, honing your planning techniques, and defining your goals at each time horizon, it is important to think about the role our devices and digital distractions play in your life. A specific survey of your tech use might even warrant its own line item in your monthly or seasonal review.

Getting personal for a moment, I have had to very deliberately step away from addictive forms of social media multiple times. In 2016, I signed off Facebook for the last time—the political infighting was stressful, and I also found myself sucked into hours of browsing on various "group" pages, reading about topics that were interesting on the surface level but added no real value to my life. In 2021, my challenge was to quit Instagram. At that point, I had been podcasting for a while but did not enjoy playing the social media game; it was so easy to "compare and despair" while looking at perfectly curated accounts of others, and as with Facebook, scrolling seemed to turn moments into hours at an alarming clip. Most recently, I had to come to terms with a Reddit fixation, though it wasn't quite as severe (I guess I had learned something from the prior two rounds!). As a creator, making the decision to avoid social media entirely felt a bit risky and subversive, but I figured that if I found the platforms fairly toxic, I didn't really want to be contributing to them, anyway. I have no regrets and have no plans to rejoin! (In case you're wondering, it's true: I have little idea what many of my high school and college acquaintances are up to. It turns out that this is not actually a problem! I have stayed in touch with the people I want to remain in touch with, and this has probably resulted in deeper relationships overall. It also makes reunions a lot more interesting!)

Each time I quit, I used my own planning tactics to my advantage.

I generally made this a focus for a given season, and often sought accountability by telling others. I used the technique of visioning mentioned in the annual planning chapter, thinking about how I would use downtime in other ways that felt calmer and healthier for me. Then, I got concrete, wrote out a manifesto (never underestimate the power of a good manifesto!) and planned these alternative activities in, sometimes directly on the calendar. "Read novel and nap on the couch" is a common Saturday afternoon list item and calendar entry for me. Quite the wild lifestyle, I know! But having a plan for something relaxing other than scrolling helps me avoid the time suck of browsing haphazardly.

There is a number of excellent books about changing your relationship with technology out there, since this is such a common struggle. If you'd like to delve deeper into this area, I am partial to Cal Newport's *Digital Minimalism*, Jonathan Haidt's *The Anxious Generation,* and Catherine Price's *How to Break Up with Your Phone.*

Challenge #6: All-or-Nothing Thinking

"I don't want to plan out every single moment!"

"I tend to go on vacation, fall off the wagon of any system I set up, and then it's all downhill from there."

"It's unrealistic for me to spend time every single day planning things out. Some days just don't go as planned, and when that happens I often have to hit the ground running and don't get to stop until I crash into bed at night."

This has some similarity to perfectionism, but with a twist: being stuck in all-or-nothing thinking about planning can mean missing out on so many benefits by assuming one has to make a choice between adhering perfectly to a given system and abandoning it altogether.

Let's take the scenario of vacation. Personally, I love planning out my day, and I do it as a matter of routine most of the time (weekdays *and* weekends), but even I often skip my daily planning rituals on vacation. Why? I just don't find them as helpful or necessary on days where my primary goals and activities are already laid out for me. Perhaps we have a day of skiing and then a fun dinner scheduled, and the only real goal on my agenda is to relax and enjoy the time with family. I might glance at my calendar or weekly list from time to time, but I can let daily planning go for a bit without issue—so I do. Now, there's nothing wrong with continuing to plan on days like this—perhaps it would be a nice reminder to be grateful about the day ahead—but it's perfectly reasonable and will not negatively impact your overall system if there are some blank pages in your paper planner or digital scheduling app.

When you get back, you can simply pick up where you left off by reviewing the last weekly list you created, giving yourself some extra time to catch up with accumulated inputs, since that post-vacation inbox can be a bit gnarly! You'll migrate or abandon undone tasks from the last week you planned out, and complete your regular weekly planning session going forward.

This approach works with longer breaks as well! Perhaps you're in the throes of morning sickness and you just have to take an elongated pause on…well, everything. When you start to feel better (for me, it was week sixteen or so) you can come up for air and begin a new seasonal list, starting from wherever you left off. You can then resume your processes at each time horizon as they come up, perhaps adjusting some of your routines to match your current energy and level of planning enthusiasm.

For those who just want some days without a plan—well, that's certainly an option! A friend of mine calls these days "shouldless" days. She leads a busy life working in finance with two young kids and enjoys having days off every quarter or so where she has no expectations of herself at all. Admittedly, she does often enjoy the fruits of prior planning labor on these days—a massage is hard to come by spontaneously! But she enjoys experiencing that day without a real plan or any predetermined list of tasks to complete. This sort of day (or week, or even a longer stretch, if that's something you are seeking) can be fit into your year while still allowing you to pursue your goals in a more deliberate way most of the time. I don't believe that my friend's shouldless days detract from her productivity or life momentum in any way, and they probably add a lot of value for her in terms of sustainability and life enjoyment.

Finally, let's address the possible loss of spontaneity and serendipity when one plans systematically at each time horizon. It's true: there is a special kind of fun in wandering around and accidentally finding a restaurant with wonderful food, fantastic ambiance, and availability without a two-hour wait. Once, I had a memorable meal in Nashville with that exact magical combination, and it was truly a delight. But much more commonly, I personally have found that *not* planning, in many scenarios, leads to disappointment. As a physician, if I don't block my time off well in advance, I won't have availability to enjoy vacation with my family without disappointing and disrupting the lives of multiple patients. If, on a Saturday night, we don't make a dinner reservation for our family of five, we end up driving around to multiple venues only to find long wait times and settling for food we weren't in the mood for. (When you're craving sushi, nothing else hits quite the same!) If I don't sign up for the race I want to run, it might sell out. If I don't plan my training for said race, I won't enjoy the experience. I could definitely go on, but my hot take on spontaneity is that while it can be fun in special circumstances, it is generally overrated and pales in comparison to the massive benefits of planning ahead.

I recognize this might seem harsh to some, but I also want to note that even with a lot of planning, there is *still* room for life to present you with positive surprises! I certainly didn't plan to meet my future husband on a camping trip before medical school, but it happened! I never expected my career to include writing or podcasting. (I mean, back when I was thinking about my career options, who knew podcasting was going to even be a thing?!) You can also strategically engineer opportunities for spontaneity in the right circumstances, like that dinner I mentioned in Nashville—my husband and I were there with no kids during the offseason and had plenty of time to spare, so it was an ideal time to wander and allow ourselves to be swept up by serendipity.

From uncertain times to planning privilege, this chapter covered a lot of ground addressing common struggles in building and maintaining one's planning system. In the next chapter, we'll peel back the curtain and let you see how real people adopt elements of this system and make it their own.

Case Studies in Planner Peace

Many planning methods are introduced in this book, and while there are certain key pieces that are nonnegotiable (a reliable master calendar, for example!), there are many areas ripe for customization. I acknowledge there are also a fair number of moving parts, and it can be useful to show how these parts can synergize and gel into a cohesive life-management system.

One of the best ways to demonstrate this is to describe the systems of several individuals who have honed their own personalized versions over time, and this chapter includes "Planner Peace" vignettes from those in various stages of life who are doing just that! Each vignette included here was submitted directly to me, with a few edits just to keep the language consistent. Some of these people have taken my courses and others have pieced together various tips from podcast episodes to enhance their own already-great setups. Included are those who prefer planning digitally and at least one planner with ADHD.

My aim is not to suggest anyone copy any of these systems outright, but to show the wide variety in implementation and provide some ideas to help get you started! You will also note that some of these vignettes include practices that differ from the core tactics in this book; for example, not everyone plans seasonally, and in one example, our planner is managing quite well with *two* master calendars (!).

These differences may be helpful for some to see, as they demonstrate that not everyone has the same planning needs, and there are many elements in one's life-management system that are flexible. There are several common threads throughout, though, and these include consistency and awareness of the system itself. Each of these participants sit down regularly to plan at multiple time horizons, and each has spent time figuring out what truly works for them, adapting various elements to fit their unique needs.

Here, the words "Planner Peace" are used slightly tongue-in-cheek. The concept of Planner Peace suggests that the user of a given planner (or system) has found permanent planner perfection, but I will note that even the best system needs tweaks, adjustments, and iterations over time as the user's needs change over various seasons of life. That said, it is a catchy phrase and these examples below are snapshots of how these individuals are enjoying some Planner Peace in this moment!

Planner Peace #1

Kae, nurse working remotely and mother of two teens

Master Calendar: My master calendar is entirely digital, using Google Calendar! I have a main calendar just for me, a shared family calendar color coded by person, a calendar for my workouts, a meal planning calendar, and a time-block calendar. My kids' sports teams are often on shared digital calendars as well, so I reference those frequently to update my own and keep them hidden otherwise. The kids and my husband all have the calendar app on their phones and reference the family calendar frequently. It also syncs to a big screen on our refrigerator door so we can all see it in the kitchen. I keep work events separate on a different digital platform, but often on Fridays I will do a reconciliation and add the next week's upcoming meeting schedule, noting generic entries like "meeting" to maintain workplace confidentiality on my personal calendar.

Airtight Task Management Methods: I use Google Tasks as my primary tool for task management, with three main lists: today, this week, and upcoming (for tasks farther out than a week, but still coming up soon). All tasks without a defined time frame go on a category-specific list, such as "household" or "kids." Every week and sometimes more frequently, I audit these lists and move things up or down in priority as needed. Every morning, I review my "this week" list and choose tasks for my daily list.

Larger-Scale Planning Rituals: I set my annual goals at the end of December and spend time identifying windows for travel and strategizing about when to use paid time off. Seasonally, I love making summer fun lists and detailed holiday task lists. Monthly, I check in with my annual goals list at the beginning of each month.

Daily and Weekly Planning Strategies: Every week and sometimes more frequently, I audit my tasks lists and move things up or down in priority as needed. I conduct a weekly planning session on Friday afternoons or Saturday mornings, which includes a detailed calendar review and update. I also look at all of my task lists to identify and note priorities for the upcoming week. My weekly ops include creating a meal plan, processing my email inbox (aiming for Inbox Zero—though it doesn't always happen!), and scheduling the next week's workouts on the calendar.

Every morning, I review my calendar, double-checking with my work calendar to make any updates, if needed. Then, I consult my task lists and choose items for my daily list. Ideally, I will choose three or four main tasks to add to my "do today" list. On weekdays, I often create a time-block plan that details my activities for the day; I add this to a separate Google Calendar to reference periodically throughout the day.

Unique Planning Tactics: I love tracking things in general! I have a digital habit-tracker spreadsheet where I check off various daily and weekly habits; it's usually the very first thing I do when I sit down in the morning. I also track my time on a spreadsheet, which has become a really fun way to journal and capture life highlights. At the end of the week, I add three to five photos to this sheet. This practice has been a great way to memory-keep and cultivate a deeper awareness of my daily activities at the same time.

Planner Peace #2

Lani, stylist, business owner, and mother of two, with ADHD diagnosed in adulthood

Master Calendar: I use Google Calendar as my master calendar—it is a precise source of truth for me regarding both work- and home-related events, and it is the most ruthlessly maintained of all of my systems! One category is named "family" and includes everything personal and family-related, from school events to my kids' sports practices to doctor's appointments and beyond. Then, I have separate calendars for my business, which I can toggle on and off to view the layers as needed. Each team member has their own calendar and color, which makes it easy to see who is doing what; mine is a pleasing shade of lavender! Finally, we have a calendar for all team members for events that impact everyone. I can view as many of these overlapping calendars as I need to at any one time.

Airtight Task Management Methods: I use a paper planner (the ProAction Planner, which I discovered via the *Best Laid Plans* podcast) to write my weekly tasks at the top of each weekly spread by category. This usually happens on Sunday evenings; during these planning sessions, I also take the time to identify tasks for Monday, and I add them to the checklist area for that day.

Throughout the week, I will select more tasks from my weekly list or bring forward undone tasks from a prior day. In order to bring lots of attention to tasks that are migrated, I highlight them—this way I can see undone tasks clearly and the highlighting helps to add a bit of a sense of urgency!

On a larger scale, I keep various lists in Apple Notes, which is easily accessible on my phone. Here, I periodically do a comprehensive brain dump and list cleanup; this ensures that less time-defined tasks are brought to the surface as needed and bigger ideas are saved for the long term.

Larger-Scale Planning Rituals: I really crave a structured and social planning experience, so I have done this for the past two years at Best Laid Plans Live (an annual guided planning retreat held in

November). After some deep reflection and planning time at the retreat, I typically stay a bit longer to solidify my goals and set up my paper planner for the upcoming year.

In addition to the traditional annual reflection and goal setting, I've added on a practice of creating a blank list of one hundred fun things in my planner to be filled in whenever I do something fun, from getting a massage to watching a movie with my kids. This simple practice has led to many fond memories and often a deeper appreciation of these happy moments.

On the seasonal level, I tend to focus on challenges coming up in the following season. One practice that has been life-changing is setting up a camp spreadsheet each summer, with the weeks in rows and my kids' names in each column, an idea Laura Vanderkam shared many years ago. Thinking through this well in advance of signups has been incredibly helpful. At the monthly level, my paper planner has built-in features that encourage me to stop and reflect each month. When I can, I identify goals for the next month and also try to appreciate highlights from the previous month.

Daily and Weekly Planning Strategies: As noted in the task-management section, I fill out my weekly planner each Sunday for the upcoming week. I always start with migrating any undone tasks from the week before, and then I update the week's calendar (with my master calendar as a reference) and select tasks for the upcoming week, with a scan of my annual goals as a reference and to remind me of my highest priorities. Weekly ops include adding in my exercise plan strategically, keeping the rest of my schedule in mind.

For family communication, we use a whiteboard with mixed

success; ultimately, I plan on having the kids primarily referencing our electronic calendar, since it's easily shared and they are at the age where they are starting to regularly carry phones.

Each day, I start my morning by reviewing the week's task list, with special attention to tasks that have gone undone over recent days. Then, I select my tasks for the day and add them to that day's column in my planner. I consider whether anything can be delegated and identify the items that need the most immediate attention. Finally, I audit my master calendar to ensure nothing has changed; if I find anything, I'll figure out how to make any necessary adjustments.

Unique Planning Tactics: One unique practice that has been incredibly helpful for my business (Real Life Style, a styling firm based in DC) has been to hold Monday morning group meetings that are primarily dedicated to planning and schedule coordination. During this meeting, we look at client appointments on the calendar for the current week and several weeks out, often a month or more. We make sure schedules and calendars are aligned to respect the time constraints of each team member and to ensure everyone has adequate space to get work done. We even review contingency plans in case childcare falls through or the city gets shut down by snow and conduct a review of open tasks and responsibilities to ensure everyone knows what is expected of them for the week ahead.

This organized approach has led to success in the business and a happy and stable team! I have also learned which tactics and habits really help mitigate some of my ADHD-related tendencies. One such habit is my practice of handwriting my appointments into my paper planner even though I have them captured electronically in my master calendar. I do this weekly, and then update it daily as needed. This pen-to-paper tactile approach really ensures the time-sensitive aspects of the day are truly set in my brain, and it prevents me from missing anything! It is incredibly important for me to be responsible and respectful of others' time in my leadership and client-facing roles, and this simple practice has made a huge difference.

In addition, I found that regularly using a detailed weekly planner spread with space to organize tasks and appointments has been a game changer for me. Previously, I tended to compartmentalize personal and work, which led to frustrating double-booking! Related to my ADHD, I also tend to succumb to the temptation of putting an entirely unrealistic number of tasks on my weekly list; having actual space limitations on a paper weekly spread helps immensely.

Planner Peace #3

Mark, father of two and IT project manager

Master Calendar: I use the Apple Calendar app as my master calendar to keep track of personal and family events. The app doesn't sync with my work calendar, but that's okay, because my wife and I send each other calendar invites about any meetings before or after typical working hours or that require driving to a different location than usual. We also send invites about anything kid-related, as well as plans that would impact our family schedule. This way we both have up-to-date master calendars and stay on the same page!

Airtight Task Management Methods: I do this digitally as well, currently using the Apple Reminders app that syncs conveniently with various devices, including my phone and iPad. I keep all of my tasks in a single list with some strategic usage of tags and filters.

My email inbox serves as a secondary task holding area, and I try to achieve Inbox Zero as often as possible. If something is time sensitive or requires a detailed response, I'll also create a task in Reminders and leave the email unread in my inbox.

Work tasks are handled separately, with my work email inbox (Outlook) serving as the primary tool for task management. I prefer this separation, and it works well for me.

Larger-Scale Planning Rituals: Annual planning has always been my favorite. I love setting and thinking about goals year-round, but especially as things are winding down around the holidays and with the fresh-start energy of the new year. For years, I've structured my annual goals around the idea of yearly themes, a concept I attribute to Myke Hurley and CGP Grey, cohosts of the *Cortex* podcast.[1] I've enjoyed the structured annual planning process within Best Laid Plans at Home (four-hour planning course); I plan on using some version of this going forward into future years. One thing I've increasingly realized about myself is that having some external accountability really helps me stick with goals and follow through on my intentions.

I store my annual goals list in the Reminders app, along with the longer-term habits and tasks that I'm managing at the daily and weekly levels. I tag anything related to my annual goals with a hashtag and the year, and this way I can filter by this tag to view my goals throughout the year.

On the topic of longer-term goal setting: Once, I tried to set a five-year goal. It didn't work!

Daily and Weekly Planning Strategies: My daily planning routine usually occurs first thing in the morning and is centered around reviewing any tasks I have scheduled for that day in the Reminders app. I'll review my schedule as well as the list and quickly decide which of the tasks seems feasible to tackle that day and which should be deferred to the next day or later in the week. Often, I'll have to adjust my list throughout the day, depending on how things are going. It's also satisfying to revisit the list to cross tasks off once they are complete!

My weekly planning is essentially an extension of my daily planning ritual, since I'm regularly moving tasks to the next day or a day later in the week. This is a bottom-up approach as opposed to the top-down approach in the nested goals system, but right now it works for me!

There are some weekly ops rituals that are usually conducted jointly with my wife, like shopping for groceries and meal planning. We have regular discussions about upcoming work and family logistics, but don't typically do them at a set time. As noted previously, I also try to reach Inbox Zero with my email and conduct broader reviews of my calendar and task list. These things generally happen at least once a week, though not at any specific time.

Unique Planning Tactics: Even though my main systems are digital, I have experimented in recent years with various paper planning products, including Hobonichi planners, hardcover Moleskine notebooks, and the Theme System Journal created by Myke Hurley and CGP Grey. I embrace digital platforms for my calendar and task management, but I've learned that I still prefer paper for certain kinds of brainstorming, notes, journaling, and memory-keeping.

I love talking with friends and family about goals, planning, and anything along those lines! But one of my favorite times to do this is with my wife, when we're on a road trip with the family, especially around the December holidays and in the summer. These conversations end up being such valuable connection points, and they also help us solidify goals and plan ahead for future travel and family adventures.

Planner Peace #4

Megan, general manager at a large company and mother to three school-aged children

Master Calendar: I use my digital work calendar (Outlook) for both work and life—it serves as my one source of truth! Work events are populated automatically, and I add everything personal so I can see it all, from the kids' field trips to time-sensitive reminders. We also have a monthly wall calendar at home to update the family on bigger events; this takes just ten minutes per month to update and serves as a nice physical reminder of what we have going on.

Airtight Task Management Methods: For tasks tethered to a specific date or time, I use the Reminders feature tethered to my digital calendar on Outlook. To capture incoming items in a place I know I will see, I often email myself, because I know for sure I will process it appropriately that way! To capture task lists related to meetings, I'll often create a simultaneous calendar event and list topics I want to address during the meeting or agenda items I don't want to forget.

Larger-Scale Planning Rituals: My introduction to annual planning was through an hour-long session taught by Sarah three years ago, and since then my annual planning time has expanded and become more detailed, including my first experience at Best Laid Plans Live last November! I enjoy having a facilitated experience to help me think through my priorities and select goals, and then I will spend some time refining those choices closer to the end of the year.

Throughout the year, I keep a master spreadsheet that includes my annual goals categorized by topic, with tabs for monthly goals as well! This year, I added more concrete steps to some of my yearly goals to make them more tactical and less vague. Each month, I select goals and identify areas of focus for the month, recording them all on the monthly section of my spreadsheet. I track habits there as well, including strength workouts, step data, meditation, and high-intensity cardio time.

Daily and Weekly Planning Strategies: Every Friday afternoon, I have a thirty-minute meeting blocked on my calendar reserved for my weekly planning time. I review the week ahead, with special attention to meetings. I determine whether there are any to cancel, shorten, or move to walking meetings, and then I write these down into a weekly planner. While they're represented on my digital calendar (master calendar!), I find that the practice of writing them in helps me think through the week. I identify any necessary prep work and list out my priorities and add both of these to my digital calendar in time blocks.

For my personal planning, I consult my master calendar and write scheduled events into my weekly planner. Then, I review my monthly spreadsheet, check off and celebrate anything completed, and select priorities and tasks for the next week. My weekly ops include scheduling workouts and planning out activities for the upcoming weekend, plus sketching out plans for the weekend after. Fun fact: my friends have learned my planning habits and expect to hear from me on Fridays with ideas of when to get together!

Unique Planning Tactics: Beyond annual and monthly goals, I have added a slew of helpful tabs to my life-management spreadsheet. I have a tab for tracking health expenses and reimbursement, a tab for our family's quarterly financials, a tab for books I want to read, and several more. It has been fun to grow this working document, and I find it incredibly useful to have as a scaffold and reference!

Planner Peace #5

Elisabeth, part-time project manager and mother of two

Master Calendar: My master calendar and most of my planning is on paper. I have tried digital tools, but I always end up back with a pen, notably the Pilot Juice Up, which Sarah recommended to me! For the past four years, I've used a spiral-bound paper weekly planner (Sprouted is the brand), and it's worked incredibly well. This planner contains all of my time-bound appointments and deadlines, plus I use it to track habits, lists, and much more. I also have a small calendar on my desk where I record work deadlines and reminders. These are also present in my master calendar, but I like having this additional reference that contains only tasks to focus on during the workday.

Airtight Task Management Tactics: The same weekly planner holds my tasks! I incorporate a weekly to-do list into the two-page spread, dividing this list into two parts, one for home and one for work.

If something has a definite deadline, I will write it as a scheduled event on the corresponding date; if there's a time-sensitive deadline, I'll go one step further and highlight it in yellow. To avoid getting stuck, I try to break onerous tasks into smaller chunks and assign myself a small window of time to get started, so it isn't so intimidating.

I keep my tasks in one of two places: my planner and my email. I only remove items from email inboxes when they've either been completed or dealt with, or if I've noted the task and any associated deadline in my paper planner. Sometimes I will send myself action items via email because I know they will reliably remain there until completion. I rarely make it to Inbox Zero, but that doesn't stop me from trying!

In terms of migrating unfinished tasks in my planner, on Sundays I look at my list and anything incomplete is triaged into three categories: no longer matter (let go), must happen next week (added to next week's list), or can happen sometime in the future (noted elsewhere).

Larger-Scale Planning Rituals: Each year, I start a period of reflection and planning around November. It's a departure from the nested goals framework, but I prefer not setting specific goals for the year. However, we sometimes sit down as a family to brainstorm adventures we'd like to experience together.

I definitely conduct fairly detailed planning sessions for each season, which is important as each season really has its own character, living as I do in eastern Canada! I pay particular attention to summer (all those camps!) and the winter holiday season; I have a Christmas spreadsheet that I use each year that includes notes about what worked well, tweaks on beloved traditions, and even a go-to grocery list of ingredients to have on hand.

Each month, I have a list of recurring tasks that I keep in a specific area of my planner's monthly spread. These include updating our family budget, various cleaning tasks, and making various payments. I consult my list each time so I don't miss anything! I also write out a list of monthly demerits and gold stars, a concept I took from Gretchen Rubin's work.[2] I find this practice helpful in identifying habits I need to tweak and to remind me to celebrate the things that are going well. Over time, I've made some significant life changes brought to light by repeated demerits.

Daily and Weekly Planning Strategies: I do most of my weekly planning on Sunday evenings. I review the upcoming calendar in detail and identify weekly tasks, adding to the "home" and "work" lists on the weekly spread. I always look back at the previous week to migrate any undone tasks forward—this ensures nothing gets left behind!

I spend some time daily consulting my planner to identify tasks for the day, and I often draw out a list in a simple white notepad. On particularly chaotic days, I'll write out any time-sensitive events and identify must-do tasks and lower -priority items.

I also have a daily ritual of completing a one-line-a-day journal! I use this as a factual diary and am amazed at how many details from the day I can capture on just a few small lines. I love reading old entries before bed.

Unique Planning Tactics: My absolute favorite place to plan is at a specific local coffee shop—I find just being in that space elevates any planning experience. My planning must-haves include a good pencil case, highlighters, a white-out pen, and a ruler; conveniently, the planner I use has one that clips right into it.

Aesthetics really matter to me! I think a beautiful planner with thick, luxe paper makes me far more excited to plan. While I don't doodle or use stickers, I still come to think of my planner as a work of art.

Planner Peace #6

A. W. Thompson, attorney and mother of one daughter with complex medical needs

Master Calendar: I don't have just one master calendar, but I do have a reliable and comprehensive calendar management system spread between two. My work system doesn't readily support syncing with external systems, and given that I don't want to think about work when I'm not at work, I've never wanted to merge my work calendar with my personal calendar. Because my role requires me to be available for on-demand meetings throughout the day, often scheduled by others during open blocks of time, one tactic I've used regularly is to block out protected select stretches of time on my work calendar—one block for lunch, and two blocks per week for my office gym sessions.

In my home life, I share multiple digital (Google) calendars with my husband. I can see his personal calendar and a pared- down version of his work calendar that only shows his work meetings that he absolutely cannot move. This way, I can view his availability when we schedule our daughter's medical appointments and school IEP meetings.

Finally, our daughter has multiple (Google) calendars that we manage related to her complex medical needs. One calendar tracks her school dates, another has her therapy and activity calendar, and a third tracks her medication adjustments. In addition to serving as a reference for me, her caregivers can access these calendars, including her grandmother and au pair. If I'm personally responsible for drop-off or pick-up or I'll be attending one of her sessions, these commitments are added to my personal calendar as well.

The key reason having multiple calendars works for me is that it's very clear (and time based!) when I need to consult which calendar. My work role is a standard nine-to-five job, so during those hours, I have my work calendar open. If the opportunity for a personal event pops up during the workday, I know my work calendar is the one I need to check to confirm my availability. All personal events during work hours are added to my work calendar, and all work events outside of nine to five are added to my personal calendar.

Airtight Task Management Tactics: Much of my task management happens during my weekly planning session (detailed in the weekly section), and I capture tasks primarily on my weekly planner spread during that time.

Larger-Scale Planning Rituals: I have always loved making annual goals, though I try to keep my process simple and streamlined. I have a small notebook that I use as the central repository for my annual goals and will begin listing ideas in this book over the last few months of the year. Then, I'll spend about an hour toward the end of the year to create a finalized list. During this session, I'll review ideas that came up earlier and brainstorm some additional ideas by category; personal, home, relationships, work, and financial are common categories from year to year, though others come into play when I feel called to include them. A "fun" category has made an appearance in recent years, for example. This session doesn't take long, as this is the one time in my year I make decisions very intuitively rather than analytically. I feel energized or drained as I think about each possible goal, and I keep the goals I feel energized about—it's that simple. Some years I've ended the process without any definitive goals, and other years I have twenty-seven!

I've never regretted skipping goal setting in the years when I knew I had no energy to place additional demands on myself—and in the years when I've felt ready to push myself, I've accomplished a ton. Some years start off very well in terms of what I'm able to do, and I wear myself out and let myself do nothing for the rest of the year. All of these scenarios are successful years to me.

Beyond yearly planning, I plan on the monthly level when I have annual goals I want to address on a monthly basis. One year, I had three goals that I wanted to happen every month: two date nights with my husband, a gym date with my dear friend from law school, and hosting a gathering at home once a month. Each month, I reviewed my calendar at the beginning of the month to decide when they should happen in order to make sure they did.

Notably, one of the most significant ways my planning is different in this current phase of my life is that my planning is driven by the energy I have available. Compared to when I was younger, I'm now more mindful of how my energy ebbs and flows. I've tried planning more routine things on a monthly level, and I find myself feeling burned out if I do it for more than two or three months. For now, aside from planning out annual goals I want to track on a monthly level, I will do monthly planning only if I'm feeling energized to do so. If I'm in the right space energetically, planning to, over the course of a month, tackle a few goals can really light me up and propel me forward. I find I typically have a few bursts a year where I accomplish many of the things on my annual goals in quick succession. Working with my energy in mind feels like I'm moving through my goals with ease rather than gritting my teeth and muscling my way through.

Daily and Weekly Planning Strategies: My weekly planning routine is the key element of my overall system and the one I do every week without fail. Because I keep my work and personal calendars separate, it's during my weekly planning session that I put everything together.

Every weekend, I sit down and review the upcoming week on all of my calendars, and I'll write my schedule out on my paper planner. Writing it out helps me to think through the mechanics of the week and scratches the itch I have to actually put pen to paper and write in a highly digital world. While writing things out, I make sure that there are no conflicts and any personal events happening during the work week are blocked off, including travel times. It's rare that there are conflicts, but if there are, catching them over the weekend means there is still enough time for me to reschedule without any negative consequences.

Once the week is set, I decide when I'll exercise and add that to the calendar. Then, I figure out which tasks I want to accomplish during the week based on the time I have available for them. If I have administrative tasks in my personal life that have to happen during work hours, I schedule a block of time on my work calendar—this not only protects this time from being taken over by others, but it also reminds me to actually do it! I also consider my likely energy levels. If it's a week with medical appointments, major work deadlines, or evening events, I'm unlikely to accomplish much else that week so I avoid adding extra or nonessential tasks to my list.

As for daily planning, I am currently without a regular daily planning practice. Pre-pandemic, when I worked at the office four days a week, I would do my daily planning on the train. Even though I'm back at the office fairly frequently, the shift to remote work really undermined my routine. It was really helpful, and I recognize that I'm less efficient many days without it, but I haven't yet been able to build it back up. If I do find I'm juggling a lot on a particular day, jotting down a game plan helps me to feel organized and focused as I move throughout the day. I'm sure daily planning will make a comeback someday.

Unique Planning Tactics: When I was twenty-nine, my college girlfriends and I shared lists of forty things we wanted to accomplish before we turned forty. Every few years, we'd have a big email chain with everyone updating the group about the progress we were making. I've loved the connection with my college friends, and I'm surprised how many things on my list I accomplished without ever really trying. Like with annual goals, I think there's something about planting the idea in my subconscious that propels me toward accomplishing the goal, even without me actively thinking about it. I'm going to make a similar list for turning fifty, and I'm definitely including audacious and ambitious goals.

Conclusion

If you feel inspired by the planners in this chapter and are ready to start building or tweaking your own system, this book served its intended purpose. I want everyone to feel excited to plan and to give your own planning processes the thought and energy they truly deserve, spawning the meta-planning revolution put forth in the introductory pages of this book.

As a very green but enthusiastic medical student learning about motivational interviewing, I ended a conversation with a faux patient (actor) pretending to be an elderly veteran coming to me for advice on how to quit smoking with: "See? That's the secret to this whole thing!"

What, exactly, was this incredibly valuable secret? No one remembers, including me. But since then, this infamous exchange has become a celebrated family joke; the idea that there's just one secret to this whole thing we call life (and that a twenty-two-year-old medical student somehow knew exactly what that was!) is so optimistic and sweet but also hilarious and ridiculous.

More than twenty years older and possibly wiser, I want to make it clear that I still don't know the secret to this whole thing. I recognize that planning can't solve everything. Sad things will still occur, illness and injustice will happen. Not everything you envision will come to fruition, and the resulting wave of disappointment can be painful and sad. But at the same time, I do know that for many people, these systems and techniques—wielded with care and intention—help a whole lot.

A comprehensive and well-maintained calendar helps you to eliminate conflicts before they cause stress and empowers you to ensure there is enough room for getting things done, resting well, and having fun.

Airtight task management helps you to be clear-eyed about exactly what is on your plate, so you can assign tasks accordingly and align your actions with your true priorities.

Clear planning processes at every time horizon (from the day to the year!) help you to move forward in the direction of your dreams one step at a time, with plenty of room to iterate and adjust along the way.

The end product of all of this isn't an artfully completed masterpiece of a planner, an empty inbox, or a series of checked-off boxes. It's a life well lived and truly enjoyed, as all of this together enables you to do more of what truly matters to you during your precious time on this earth.

Checklist for Your Complete System

Master Calendar

☐ Create one reliable calendar that integrates all of the time-specific events you need to know about in one place.

☐ Define calendar maintenance rituals, including:

- Immediately recording anything time specific you are committing to in the future (as you commit, it goes directly in the calendar!)
- Regularly auditing sneaky input sources to ensure your data is complete
- Sharing with others in a strategic manner

Airtight Task Management

☐ Develop a clear list of all of your active inboxes (just a few examples: physical mailbox, work email, school WhatsApp thread).

☐ Define when, where, and how often you will process these inboxes (either to empty with traditional Inbox Zero, or to your version of 100 percent current).

☐ Process each item asking five key questions, and capture or file away the input based on your triage:

- Is this a task to assign myself?
- Does this message represent a calendar item I need to note somewhere?
- Is this a piece of information I will need to see at a specific time (i.e., on a trip, or just before a meeting)?
- Is this item something that is not time specific, but that feels important enough to store outside of just archiving it?

- Do I need to take time to write a detailed response?

☐ Process tasks into the following categories:

- Tether to a specific day/date (add to calendar).
- Add to current weekly list.
- Add to a future week's list (or a "do soon" list, if you prefer that strategy).
- Add to an "after the storm" list, if you're in a period of overwhelm.
- Add to a someday possibilities list, if you're not ready to assign the task a time frame, but want to hold on to it.

☐ Set up digital filing system to create an easily searchable database of reference material.

Nested Goals System

Annual Planning

☐ Identify and schedule a time and place for annual planning to take place, ideally spread out over at least two half days.

☐ Conduct an annual planning retreat with the following elements:

- Visioning, both longer-term (five to ten years out) and for one year into the future.
- Reflect back on the previous year; celebrate wins and analyze what didn't work for you.
- Revisit your someday possibilities list, if you have one.
- Calendar landscape overview
- Goal generation, setting goals in several domains (examples: work, personal, financial, relationships, fun)

☐ During or after your retreat, audit and refine goals for balance (process vs. outcome goals; habit- and routine-related goals; ratio of obligatory vs. exciting goals).

- ☐ Save your list and consider a digital backup if it's on paper.
- ☐ Create a plan to share your goals.
- ☐ Set a date for the next time you will review your list, and add that date to your calendar.

Seasonal Planning

- ☐ Define your season (ideas: traditional quarters, trimesters, quintiles) to segment the year into three to six chunks that fit the rhythms of your life.
- ☐ Block time in your calendar for about a half day's worth of planning and reflection; consider conducting your seasonal planning with a friend or partner.
- ☐ During your session:
    - Reflect back on the last season, celebrating victories and noting incomplete goals; decide what you'd like to migrate forward and if there's anything you feel ready to let go.
    - Review your annual goals list and your someday possibilities list if it feels like you are open to more ideas.
    - Look ahead, around, and within: acknowledge the realities of your upcoming calendar, the demands of the season, and your own energy levels and mood.
    - Generate seasonal goals list in several domains.
        Identify and note the next action for multi-step projects.
    - Add key time-sensitive tasks directly to your calendar.
    - Complete the Ideal Week exercise.

- Conduct a seasonal financial assessment.
- Plan in various "wild card" areas based on current life needs (examples: childcare, travel, household maintenance, work meetings, wardrobe, media, meal planning).

☐ Decide on your next seasonal planning session and add it to your calendar.

Monthly Planning

☐ Block off about two hours each month for your monthly session.

☐ Find ways to celebrate the start of the month (examples: new phone background; new color scheme in your planner).

☐ During your session:

- Review your seasonal goals list, last month's goals, the upcoming calendar landscape, and your own interior mood and energy.
- Based on those lists, generate goals for the month in several domains.
- Reflect on habits and identify any habits of focus for the month.
- Complete a fun audit!
- Monthly Life Maintenance—add in as they may apply (examples: bill paying, paper management, decluttering, household supply audit, errands and appointments).

☐ Decide on the next monthly session and add it to your calendar.

Weekly Planning

☐ Identify a standard time slot for your weekly planning.

- Ensure you also have adequate time for any associated inbox processing.

☐ During your session:

- Reflect and review the last week's accomplishments and undone tasks; decide what to migrate and what to let go.
- Review your monthly goals list and your upcoming calendar. Ensure your master calendar is complete and up-to-date by auditing all potential input sources.
- Ensure inboxes are processed so that you are current about what is on your plate.

  Note: for many, achieving Inbox Zero or the equivalent shortly before conducting this session is helpful.
- Assess your current mood and energy status.
- Generate your weekly tasks and record them so that they are clearly tied to the upcoming week.
- Ensure your processes include planning the weekends!

☐ Consider additional weekly ops in areas of life that apply to you (examples: wardrobe, meals, exercise, sleep, childcare, fun, other household tasks, spiritual practice, media, finances).

☐ Develop a weekly communication plan, ideally a written and verbal component, with all stakeholders (your partner, your kids, your coworkers, if any apply).

Daily Planning

☐ Identify a regular time in your day (ten to fifteen minutes) for conducting your daily planning session.

☐ During your session:

- Look back on the prior day to ensure all notes and incomplete tasks have been processed appropriately.

- Review your master calendar, checking for last-minute changes or add-ons; create or view a timeline of the day's scheduled events.
- Check in with your energy and mood.
- Review your weekly task list.
- Create a realistic list of tasks for the day, selecting items that fit the day's time constraints and your energy, while prioritizing urgent needs.

☐ Throughout the day, check in with yourself regarding habits you aim to complete daily; track these in a way that feels right to you.

☐ Consider a closing ritual at the end of each day, processing undone tasks, celebrating progress, and setting yourself up for success in the morning.

☐ Try time-block planning (defining your tasks at each minute of the workday) on packed days.

☐ Remain ready to pivot and iterate—some days will not go exactly as planned, and that's okay and expected!

Acknowledgments

This book started out as a dream on my own someday possibilities list, and it probably would have stayed there if it wasn't for the support of everyone on this page.

Huge thanks to my editor Ariel Curry, who reached out and lit a fire to finally get me moving forward with this big, daunting project, as well as the rest of the amazing team at Sourcebooks who put their faith in a first-time author. I also want to thank Rebecca Andersen, Emily Proano, and Ellina Litmanovich for their careful copy editing and proofreading.

From the earliest days of this project, I want to thank Jessica Johnson Webb for her original organization of the content and Lizzy Fox for her wonderful graphics work. I also want to acknowledge Ashton Renshaw who assisted with some of those last-minute details.

Thank you to Phyllis and Kelvin Nichols from Sound Advice Strategies, who have always come through with my podcast episode production.

To my friends that have been following along in this process and offering their wisdom and advice (Kelsey Wharton and Kelly Nolan on our phone dates and Kaelyn Lopez on our constant text chats), I so appreciate you listening to me and lifting me up! And of course, huge thanks to Laura Vanderkam for her ideas, her friendship, and for always giving me confidence to try things.

I am grateful for every one of my course participants (live and virtual!)—you all bring such wonderful energy and have taught me so much. Special shout-out to Amanda W., Lani, Mark, A. W., Elisabeth, and Megan for submitting Planner Peace segments for the case studies chapter!

To everyone who has read my twenty-year-old blog and commented over the years at theshubox.com—I owe so much to you, too! I love the kind and wise community that has grown in my tiny corner of the internet.

To my parents, Alex and Caryn Hart, and my parents-in-law, Beverly and Steve Unger: thank you for always being interested in my endeavors, and extra thanks to Alex for reviewing my book proposal!

To Rebecca, thank you for always being one text away. And Geeta: this book would not have been possible without your dedication and care of the kids.

To Josh, my husband of almost twenty years (!) as of this book's publication: Thank you for everything, but especially for supporting and encouraging me as I followed this unconventional career path. You are the best. Annabel, Cameron, and Genevieve: I love you and the life our family has together. I can't wait for the adventures we'll plan in the years to come.

Notes

CHAPTER 1: ESSENTIAL TOOLS

1 David Allen, "What is GTD?" Getting Things Done, accessed February 13, 2025, https://gettingthingsdone.com/what-is-gtd/.

2 David Allen, *Getting Things Done: The Art of Stress-Free Productivity* (Penguin Books, 2001), 277.

3 "Zeigarnik Effect," Simply Psychology, accessed February 13, 2025, https://www.simplypsychology.org/zeigarnik-effect.html.

4 Tiago Forte, *Building a Second Brain: A Proven Method to Organize Your Digital Life and Unlock Your Creative Potential* (Atria Books, 2022), 90.

CHAPTER 3: QUINTILES, TRIMESTERS, AND PLANNING WITHIN YOUR SEASONS

1 The Ideal Week: A Framework for Work-Life Balance," Full Focus, accessed February 13, 2025, https://fullfocus.co/ideal-week/.

2 "Mustache Calculator," MustacheCalc, accessed February 13, 2025, http://mustachecalc.com/.

3 "Courses," *The Shu Box*, accessed February 13, 2025, https://theshubox.com/courses.

4 "Home," *Rising Shining*, accessed February 13, 2025, https://www.risingshining.com/.

5 Kendra Adachi, *The Lazy Genius Kitchen: Have What You Need, Use What You Have, and Enjoy It Like Never Before* (Workman Publishing, 2022), Part 2, Area 3.

CHAPTER 4: THE MONTH, OR YOUR TWELVE YEARLY CLEAN SLATES

1 Hengchen Dai, Katherine L. Milkman, and Jason Riis, "The Fresh Start Effect: Temporal Landmarks Motivate Aspirational Behavior," *Management Science* 60, no. 10 (2014): iv-vi, 2381-2617, http://dx.doi.org/10.1287/mnsc.2014.1901.

2 Maxwell Maltz, *Psycho-Cybernetics* (Pocket Books, 1960), pp XI–XIV.

3 Phillipa Lally, Cornelia H. M. van Jaarsveld, Herry W. W. Potts, and Jane Wardle, "How Are Habits Formed: Modelling Habit Formation in the Real World," *European Journal of Social Psychology* 40, no. 6 (2009): 998-1009 https://doi.org/10.1002/ejsp.674.

4 Jodi Wellman, *You Only Die Once* (Voracious, 2024), 285.

CHAPTER 5: THE WEEK: PLAYING TIME TETRIS WITH YOUR 168 HOURS

1 David Allen, *Getting Things Done: The Art of Stress-Free Productivity*, (New York: Penguin Books, 2001), 195.

2 Gretchen Rubin, "Are You an Upholder, a Questioner, a Rebel, or an Obliger?" GretchenRubin .com, accessed February 13, 2025, https://gretchenrubin.com/articles/are-you-an-upholder -a-questioner-a-rebel-or-an-obliger/.

3 Laura Vanderkam, *Tranquility by Tuesday: 9 Ways to Calm the Chaos and Make Time for What Matters* (Portfolio, 2022), 139.

CHAPTER 6: PLANNING YOUR DAY WITH INTENTION (BECAUSE EVERY DAY COUNTS!)

1 Gretchen Rubin, "The Years Are Short," YouTube video, June 15, 2012, https://www .youtube.com/watch?v=KktuoQwb3vQ.

2 Jenny Stancampiano, "New Years Runs and Resolutions," *Runners Fly*, January 2, 2024, https://runnersfly.com/new-years-runs-and-resolutions/.

3 Jenny Stancampiano, "Mid-Year Check In Part 2," *Runners Fly*, July 9, 2024, https:// runnersfly.com/mid-year-check-in-part-2/.

4 Kelly Nolan, "Bright Method Basics," *Kelly Nolan*, May 14, 2023, https://kellynolan.com/podcast-1/.

5 Heather J. Ferguson, Victoria E. A. Brunsdon, and Elisabeth E. F. Bradford, "The Developmental Trajectories of Executive Function from Adolescence to Old Age," *Scientific Reports* 11, no. 1 (2021): https://doi.org/10.1038/s41598-020-80866-1.

6 Cal Newport, *Deep Work: Rules for Focused Success in a Distracted World* (Grand Central Publishing, 2016), 223; Cal Newport, *Time-Block Planner (Second Edition): A Daily Method for Deep Work in a Distracted World* (Portfolio, 2015).

7 David Allen, "GTD Workflow Processing and Organizing," GTD, 2014, https:// gettingthingsdone.com/wp-content/uploads/2014/10/workflow_map.pdf.

8 Huberman Lab, "Lower Stress With an End-of-Day Ritual | Dr. Cal Newport & Dr. Andrew Huberman," YouTube video, April 18, 2024, https://www.youtube.com/watch ?v=NsNA8XHbQjQ.

CHAPTER 7: WHEN YOU FIND YOURSELF STUCK—BURNOUT, OVERLOAD, BIG PROJECT INTIMIDATION, AND PROCRASTINATION

1 Kendra Adachi, *The PLAN: Manage Your Time Like a Lazy Genius*, (Convergent Books, 2024), 76–84.

2 Cal Newport, *Slow Productivity: The Lost Art of Accomplishment Without Burnout* (Portfolio, 2024), 72–75.

3 M. D. Musumeci, C. M. Cunningham, and T. L. White, "Disgustingly Perfect: An Examination of Disgust, Perfectionism, and Gender," *Motivation and Emotion* 46, no. 3 (2022): 336–49, https://doi.org/10.1007/s11031-022-09931-8.

CHAPTER 8: CHALLENGES: FROM PLANNING PRIVILEGE TO TIME SUCKS AND BEYOND

1 Lisa Woodruff, *Organization Is a Learnable Skill* (Independently Published, 2021).

2 Peg Dawson, Richard Guare, and Colin Guare, *Smart but Scattered: The Revolutionary Executive Skills Approach to Helping Kids Reach Their Potential, 2nd Edition* (Guilford Press, 2024); Peg Dawson and Richard Guare, *The Smart but Scattered Guide to Success: How to Use Your Brain's Executive Skills to Keep Up, Stay Calm, and Get Organized at Work and at Home* (Guilford Press, 2016).

CHAPTER 9: CASE STUDIES IN PLANNER PEACE

1 Myke Hurley and CGP Grey, "#62: 2018 Yearly Themes," *Cortex* podcast, January 2018, https://www.relay.fm/cortex/62.

2 Gretchen Rubin, "446: Re-Think Our Daily Routine, Recognize the Warning Signs of Obliger-Rebellion, and a Back-to-School Demerit," *Happier with Gretchen Rubin*, September 6, 2023, https://gretchenrubin.com/podcast/446-re-think-our-daily-routine-recognize-the-warning-signs-of-obliger-rebellion-and-a-back-to-school-demerit/.

About the Author

Sarah Hart-Unger is a practicing pediatric endocrinologist, writer, and podcaster with a passion for planning. She loves to share her systems and techniques with others through courses and live planning retreats. She lives with her husband and three children in South Florida. She has been writing most days for over 20 years at theshubox.com.